# The Necessity of Systematic Theology

# The Necessity of Systematic Theology

## Second Edition

JOHN JEFFERSON DAVIS, EDITOR

Baker Book House
Grand Rapids, Michigan

Copyright 1978 by
University Press of America, Inc.

Second Edition issued 1980 by
Baker Book House Company
with permission of copyright holder

ISBN: 0-8010-2903-1

*First printing, August 1980*
*Second printing, October 1983*

PHOTOLITHOPRINTED BY CUSHING - MALLOY, INC.
ANN ARBOR, MICHIGAN, UNITED STATES OF AMERICA

# Contributors

**C. S. Lewis** (1898–1963) was Professor of Medieval and Renaissance English at Cambridge University.

**R. C. Sproul** is Director and Staff Theologian at the Ligonier Valley Study Center near Stahlstown, Pennsylvania.

**John H. Gerstner** is Professor of Church History at Pittsburgh Theological Seminary.

**Dorothy L. Sayers** ((1893–1957) was an English novelist, essayist, and playwright.

**Kenneth F. W. Prior** is Vicar of St. Nicholas' Church, Sevenoaks, Kent, England.

**Robert L. Saucy** is Professor of Systematic Theology at Talbot Theological Seminary, La Mirada, California.

**Emil Brunner** (1889–1966) was Professor of Theology at Zürich University, Switzerland.

**Francis Pieper** (1852–1931) was Professor of Theology at Concordia Theological Seminary, St. Louis.

**Jonathan Edwards** (1703–1758) was a Congregational pastor in Northampton, Massachusetts, a philosopher, and theologian of the Great Awakening.

**B. B. Warfield** (1851–1921) was Professor of Didactic and Polemic Theology at Princeton Theological Seminary.

**John Jefferson Davis** is Associate Professor of Theology at Gordon-Conwell Theological Seminary.

# Contents

# Preface

This volume has grown out of a desire to make available in a more convenient form readings assigned in connection with my seminary course in prolegomena and the doctrine of God. It is hoped that the present anthology will eliminate the inevitable frustrations created by large numbers of students simultaneously seeking access to a limited number of reserve readings.

The articles reprinted here have as a common theme the value of systematic, disciplined reflection on biblical truth for Christian living and ministry. In a cultural climate which tends to stress subjective experience rather than systematic reflection, there would seem to be a particular need to set forth an explicit rationale for the study of systematic theology. The authors in this volume, whose lives span several centuries, have made such a case with a notable measure of clarity and theological insight.

I wish to express special appreciation to Corinne Witham, Corinne Languedoc and Holly Greening, who so carefully prepared the typed manuscript. My wife Robin was most helpful in terms of general encouragement and in proofreading the finished copy. I also wish to thank the administrative cabinet of Gordon-Conwell Theological Seminary for generous help with royalty fees.

I would like to thank the following authors, publishers, and copyright holders for permission to use the selections reprinted in this book: Presbyterian and Reformed Publishing Company for sections of *Studies in Theology* by B. B. Warfield; A. Watkins, Inc., for sections of *Creed or Chaos?* by Dorothy Sayers; Macmillan Publishing Co., Inc., for sections of *The Screwtape Letters* by C. S. Lewis; Concordia Publishing House for sections of *Christian Dogmatics* by Francis Pieper; Westminster Press for sections of *The Christian Doctrine of God* by Emil Brunner; Moody Press, Moody Bible Institute of Chicago, for sections of *Theology for Everyman* by John Gerstner; Theological Students Fellowship for the article "The Minister As Teacher" by Kenneth Prior; the *Journal of the Evangelical Theological Society* for the article "Doing Theology for the Church" by R. L. Saucy; R. C. Sproul for the article "Right Now Counts Forever," which appeared in *Tabletalk.*

Gordon-Conwell Theological Seminary          JOHN JEFFERSON DAVIS
South Hamilton, Massachusetts
June, 1978

*C. S. Lewis*

# 1

# The Screwtape Letters
# Letter I

My dear Wormwood,

I note what you say about guiding your patient's reading and taking care that he sees a good deal of his materialist friend. But are you not being a trifle *naïf*? It sounds as if you supposed that *argument* was the way to keep him out of the Enemy's clutches. That might have been so if he had lived a few centuries earlier. At that time the humans still knew pretty well when a thing was proved and when it was not; and if it was proved they really believed it. They still connected thinking with doing and were prepared to alter their way of life as the result of a chain of reasoning. But what with the weekly press and other such weapons, we have largely altered that. Your man has been accustomed, ever since he was a boy, to having a dozen incompatible philosophies dancing about together inside his head. He doesn't think of doctrines as primarily "true" or "false," but as "academic" or "practical," "outworn" or " contemporary," "conventional" or "ruthless." Jargon, not argument, is your best ally in keeping him from the church. Don't waste time trying to make him think that materialism is *true!* Make him think it is strong or stark or courageous—that it is the philosophy of the future. That's the sort of thing he cares about.

The trouble about argument is that it moves the whole struggle onto the Enemy's own ground. He can argue too;

whereas in really practical propaganda of the kind I am suggesting He has been shown for centuries to be greatly the inferior of Our Father Below. By the very act of arguing, you awake the patient's reason; and once it is awake, who can foresee the result? Even if a particular train of thought can be twisted so as to end in our favor, you will find that you have been strengthening in your patient the fatal habit of attending to universal issues and withdrawing his attention from the stream of immediate sense experiences. Your business is to fix his attention on the stream. Teach him to call it "real life" and don't let him ask what he means by "real."

Remember he is not, like you, a pure spirit. Never having been a human (oh, that abominable advantage of the Enemy's!) you don't realize how enslaved they are to the pressure of the ordinary. I once had a patient, a sound atheist, who used to read in the British Museum. One day, as he sat reading, I saw a train of thought in his mind beginning to go the wrong way. The Enemy, of course, was at his elbow in a moment. Before I knew where I was I saw my twenty years' work beginning to totter. If I had lost my head and begun to attempt a defense by argument, I should have been undone. But I was not such a fool. I struck instantly at the part of the man which I had best under my control and suggested that it was just about time he had some lunch. The Enemy presumably made the counter-suggestion (you know how one can never *quite* overhear what He says to them?) that this was more important than lunch. At least I think that must have been His line, for when I said, "Quite. In fact much *too* important to tackle at the end of a morning," the patient brightened up considerably; and by the time I had added "Much better come back after lunch and go into it with a fresh mind," he was already halfway to the door. Once he was in the street the battle was won. I showed him a newsboy shouting the midday paper, and a No. 73 bus going past, and before he reached the bottom of the steps I had got into him an unalterable conviction that, whatever odd ideas might come into a man's head when he was shut up alone with his books, a healthy dose of "real life" (by which he meant the bus and the newsboy) was enough to show him that all "that sort of thing" just couldn't be true. He knew he'd had a narrow escape and in later years was fond of talking about "that inarticulate sense for actuality which is our ultimate safeguard against the aberrations of mere logic." He is now safe in Our Father's house.

You begin to see the point? Thanks to processes which we set at work in them centuries ago, they find it all but impossible to believe in the unfamiliar while the familiar is before their eyes. Keep pressing home on him the *ordinariness* of things. Above all, do not attempt to use science (I mean, the real sciences) as a defense against Christianity. They will positively encourage him to think about realities he can't touch and see. There have been sad cases among the modern physicists. If he must dabble in science, keep him on economics and sociology; don't let him get away from that invaluable "real life." But the best of all is to let him read no science but to give him a grand general idea that he knows it all and that everything he happens to have picked up in casual talk and reading is "the results of modern investigation." Do remember you are there to fuddle him. From the way some of you young fiends talk, anyone would suppose it was our job to *teach!*

Your affectionate uncle
SCREWTAPE

Reprinted with permission of Macmillan Publishing Co., Inc., from *The Screwtape Letters* by C. S. Lewis. Copyright 1942 by C. S. Lewis.

# 2

# Right Now
# Counts Forever

"Never preach above an eighth–grade level to a college educated congregation . . ." These words are still echoing in my ears and stabbing me in the soul. They were uttered by my Professor of Homiletics in seminary. He was trying to teach us how to be "successful" preachers. He went on to explain that people may have college degrees in their fields of specialty but in matters of religion and theology the majority of them have no better than a Sunday school understanding. The way to success is to "keep it simple."

The way to success is to "keep it simple." Something deep within me reacted to this "advice." I refused to accept it then. I refuse to accept it now. The advice carries within it a double insult. The first insult is to God's people. To assume that adults cannot grasp the things of God beyond an eighth–grade level is to slander both their intelligence and maturity.

The second insult is far greater. It is an insult to the majesty of God and to the work of God the Holy Spirit in revealing the deep things of God for us. We will spend thousands of dollars to educate ourselves and acquire knowledge to enhance our careers. We understand the importance of knowledge in many areas of life. Our public education system does not terminate at eighth grade. We would be ill-equipped for the conversations we have in our businesses if our knowledge of the English language reached only the eighth-grade level.

What are the standard clichés that abound in the Christian community? Have you heard them? "We must have a childlike faith." "I don't need to know any theology, I just need to know Jesus." "Christianity is simple: 'Jesus loves me this I know, for the Bible tells me so.'"

It is easy for us to confuse a childlike faith with a childish faith. We are to have the kind of implicit trust in God that a child has in its parents. But we are called to fullness of maturity in terms of our understanding God. The apostle Paul put it this way: "Brethren, do not be children in your thinking; yet in evil be babes, but in your thinking be mature" (I Cor. 14:20).

To say we don't need to know theology, only Jesus, raises the immediate question, "Who is Jesus?" As soon as we begin to answer that question we are instantly involved in theology. As Christians we simply cannot avoid theology. We aren't all expected to be theologians in a technical or academic sense, but we are theologians with a small "t." The question is not will we be theologians but will we be good theologians or poor theologians?

"Jesus loves me this I know . . ." There is no more basic truth to Christianity than that. As an adult I still love to sing the song. But I also like to sing "Holy, Holy, Holy," "A Mighty Fortress Is Our God," and "Immortal, Invisible Only Wise God."

Christianity has simplicity, but it is not simplistic. The depths and riches of God are profound enough to keep us busily engaged in earnest pursuit of the knowledge of God for the rest of our lives. Its basic truths are easy enough for a child to grasp, but its deeper truths require disciplined study.

There is the famous story of the meeting of the theologian and the astronomer. The astronomer said to the theologian: "I don't understand why you theologians fuss so much about predestination and supralapsarianism, about communicable and uncommunicable attributes of God, of imputed or infused grace and the like; to me

Christianity is simple; it's the Golden Rule, 'Do unto others as you would have others do unto you.'" The theologian replied, "I think I see what you mean. I get lost in all your talk about exploding novae, expanding universes, theories of entropy and astronomical perturbations. For me astronomy is simple: It's 'Twinkle, twinkle little star. . .'"

Last week a woman said to me, "I was a Christian for eleven years before I found out who God was. It was after viewing your video series on the 'Holiness of God' that I first understood the majesty of God." She went on to say, "I suddenly felt cheap about having a bumper sticker on my car saying, 'Honk if you love Jesus.' It seemed to make God seem so small." As delighted as I was that the woman had moved to a deeper understanding of God, I tried to reassure her about her bumper sticker. She was trying to do something 'visible" to indicate her commitment to Christ. We all start our Christian walk as babes and don't always know the best way to articulate our faith. This woman wanted to go deeper.

To be satisfied with a simple faith that is maintained on a milk diet stunts your growth as a Christian. The problem is as old as the church itself. On occasion the apostles had to admonish their spiritual children on this point. We read: "Therefore, leaving the elementary teaching about the Christ, let us press on to maturity . . ." (Heb. 6:1). Again: ". . . Until we all attain to the unity of the faith, and of the knowledge of the Son of God, to a mature man, to the measure of the stature which belongs to the fullness of Christ. As a result we are no longer to be children, tossed here and there by waves, and carried about by every wind of doctrine . . ." (Eph. 4:13–14).

God wants you to be a spiritual giant. There are different ways to define the word *giant*. We would describe a giant as "a grotesque creature who is a freak of nature." We could define a giant as "a mythical character who is featured in fairy tales like 'Jack and the Beanstalk.'" But God does not want you to be a grotesque freak or a mythical person who says Fee Fi Fo Fum. . . . A spiritual giant is a different kind of giant. In this sense a giant is simply *a normal person who never quits growing.*

Christian education is an educational process that has no graduation date until we die. We may complete special or particular courses of study, but we pursue our knowledge of God as long as we live. Christian education involves a lifelong pursuit of God Himself.

The Bible speaks of seeking God. Again and again we hear the words, "Seek and ye shall find." But in almost every case where the Bible speaks of seeking after God it is speaking to and about believers. Jonathan Edwards said, "The seeking of God is the main business of my life."

It was to believers Jesus said, "Seek ye first the kingdom of God and his righteousness and all these things will be added unto you." To seek after God is to have an unquenchable thirst to know Him deeply.

Lifelong Christian education is what we pastors are striving for. We want to help you grow into giants. We want to help you learn as much as you can about the things of God. We want to make the "Seminary" available to the layman. We want to provide you with tools of knowledge of the Bible, of theology, of church history, practical aids to personal growth, to the whole gamut of Christian education.

We want you to be knowledgeable and articulate Christians, not so that you can win arguments or boast of your brilliance, but so that you can have the food you need to be a giant for God.

---

From *Tabletalk,* March, 1978. Reprinted by permission.

*John H. Gerstner*

# 3

# Everyman Must Be a Theologian

Laymen sometimes think they need not be theologians. That, however, is a very great mistake. They do need to be theologians; at least, they should be amateur theologians. In fact, that is the one vocation every man is obliged to follow. A layman does not need to be a plumber, a carpenter, a lawyer, a doctor, a teacher, a laborer, a housewife. These are all possibilities, not necessities. A layman may be one of these or the other as he chooses. But he must be a theologian. This is not an option with him but a requirement.

## A Theologian Is One Who Knows about God

Why do we say that a layman must be a theologian? Well, let us first of all realize what a theologian is—that is, an amateur theologian. A theologian is a person who knows about God. A lay theologian is a person who has a true knowledge of God, which he understands in nontechnical, nonprofessional, nonacademic terms. However, such a person is truly a theologian.

Is it not clear why a layman must necessarily be a theologian? Is there anyone, layman or otherwise, who does not need to know God? Does the Scripture not say, "This is life eternal, that they might know thee the only true God, and Jesus Christ, whom thou hast sent" (John 17:3)? It is, then, no mere option with a layman whether he will be a theologian or not, whether he will have eternal life or not; it is no option with him whether he will know God or not. The knowledge of God is necessary to eternal life. And if eternal life is necessary for every man, then theology is also necessary for every man.

If a theologian is a person who knows God, then by reverse reasoning a person who is not a theologian does not know God. There is no shame in a layman's being told that he does not know carpentry, or plumbing, or medicine, or law, or teaching, or the ways of a housewife; but there surely is the greatest of shame in a layman's being told that he does not know God. Furthermore, there is more than shame; there is a very great danger. The Scripture says that to live apart from God is death. And just as the text quoted says it is life eternal to know God and Christ, another passage in the same book says they who do not believe in Jesus shall not see life and, furthermore, the wrath of God abides upon them: "He that believeth on the Son hath everlasting life: and he that believeth not the Son shall not see life; but the wrath of God abideth on him" (John 3:36).

"Well," the layman may say, "look here, you've slipped in a new term on us. That last passage talks about faith and not knowledge. It says except a person 'believe' in the Son. It does not say anything there about 'knowing' Jesus." That is true, the passage does not use the word *know*. It does speak about "belief" or "faith" rather than "knowledge" or "reason." But have you ever believed in somebody or something about which you knew nothing? Is it possible to have faith in Christ unless we know who Christ is? Is it not clear, therefore, that this passage, though it does not state expressly the necessity of the knowledge of Christ, certainly states it implicitly? So we say that if a person does not have a knowledge of God and Christ, it is not only a shame but a peril to his soul, not only in this life but in the eternity which begins at death.

## Everyman May Be a Theologian Without Being Saved!

"But," the layman exclaims, "do you mean to tell me that if I do not have the knowledge of God I shall perish, and that if I do have the knowledge of God I will live forever? Do you mean to tell me that if I am a lay theologian all is well with my soul, whereas if I am not I am doomed forever?" No, we have not said exactly that. Let me call your attention to what we did actually say, and then let me add a comment relevant to one of your questions. We did say that without knowledge of God there is no eternal life, but only eternal death. That is true. And we did say that if we do not know God and Christ we will perish. That is true. However, it needs to be brought out now that there is knowledge and *knowledge*. The knowledge of which the Scripture speaks so approvingly we may call "saving knowledge." But we gather from other passages of Scripture which we have not yet cited that there is also a false knowledge which, far from being saving knowledge, is actually damning knowledge. But it seems to me we are now ready for a closer consideration of this theme. Let me, therefore, lay down this statement and devote the rest of this chapter to demonstrating it. The statement is this: A layman may have knowledge of God and not be saved, but he can never be saved without knowledge of God.

There is much to show that a layman may have theology without having salvation. For one thing, the Bible says in many places that frequently persons have a knowledge about God but do not know God. Thus, for example, the Scripture exhorts us to be not only hearers of the Word but doers also (cf. James 1:22).

This implies that it is possible to hear, or learn, or know, without doing. It goes on to tell us that only the doing of the Word is profitable, again carrying the implication that persons may hear the Word and understand it without actually doing it and therefore without being profitable. Again, Paul speaks in Romans of those who hold the truth in unrighteousness (1:18). That is the same as to say that some persons know God (and indeed in this very context Paul does speak of knowing God) and yet do not worship Him nor are they being saved by Him. So we learn that while their knowledge is sufficient to condemn them, they are not saved by it.

In the parable of the sower and the seed recorded in Matthew 13, our Lord tells of differing responses to the presentation of the gospel. While the wayside soil represents those persons who seem virtually not to hear what is preached, or not to learn what they are taught, still the other two types of useless soil represent persons who do hear and do understand but who nevertheless do not bring forth fruit. Thus the shallow, rocky soil does represent a person who receives the Word, as Jesus says. He receives it with gladness and even seems to respond favorably to it for a while. But when he is beset by difficulties, he repudiates the knowledge which he does have. So we see in his case an individual who knows but does not do, who understands the way of salvation but does not attain to salvation. The thorny soil represents a person who understands and accepts the message but whose knowledge is crushed out in the subsequent contest between that message and his lusts, which are represented by thorns in the soil. But there can be no doubt that he not only has knowledge but deep and penetrating and not merely superficial knowledge. Nonetheless, his knowledge is choked out and the man does not attain to salvation.

There are many other instances of the possibility of knowing the truth without being saved. But we will take one, that of the Pharisees, and use it as our prime exhibit. The layman will immediately say, "Ah, but the Pharisees were religious teachers and cannot fairly be called laymen." This we admit. But we will also go on to insist that our point is certified all the more by the fact that the Pharisees, as professional theologians, had even greater knowledge than laymen could be expected to have—and yet the Pharisees perished. Remember, we are attempting to show that it is possible to have theological knowledge without being saved. If we can show that one who is regarded as a professional (who has far more religious knowledge than a layman may be expected to have) may yet perish, how much more evident is it that any knowledge that a layman can reasonably be expected to obtain can by no means guarantee his salvation. Jesus approved of the Pharisees in many ways because they attempted to honor Moses' law—and often did—and teach his precepts to the people. However, they came under Christ's withering indictment, "Woe unto you Pharisees, hypocrites," so often that we are led to believe that as a class these highly knowledgeable individuals were not practitioners of their science and therefore were doomed to condemnation. Jesus said to them, "How can you escape the damnation of hell?" (Matt. 23:33).

## Everyman Cannot Be Saved Without Being a Theologian

If the above is enough to indicate that persons may have divine knowledge without being saved, let us go on to indicate the still more pertinent truth—that no one can be saved without the knowledge of divine truth or theology. This is stated very explicitly in Romans 10:17. Here Paul says, "Faith cometh by hearing." That is as much as to affirm that there can be no belief except first the Word of the gospel is proclaimed. The context of this explicit statement confirms that implication. It is a missionary context in which Paul is urging Christians to take the gospel to the world, reminding them that if they do not do so these people cannot be saved—because faith comes by hearing. In I Corinthians we read that it pleased God by the foolishness of preaching to save men. Again, says Paul, "I am not ashamed of the gospel of Christ: for it is the power of God unto salvation" (Rom. 1:16). And, after commanding the disciples to teach whatsoever He had taught them, our Lord Jesus commissioned them to make disciples of all nations (Matt. 28:19–10). That is the same as to say that it is by means of the faithful proclamation of the whole counsel of God that the world is to be discipled to Jesus Christ. Consider again how our Lord prays in His farewell discourse, "Sanctify them through thy truth: thy word is truth" (John 17:17). In this final prayer for those who were not yet of His fold but who were to come into His fold, our Lord prayed that they might be made holy by means of the Word of God. Though the Spirit of God was to be given anew as soon as Christ went to heaven, even the Holy Spirit was not to sanctify except by means of the Word of God. So that while the letter of the Word may be devoid of the Spirit and therefore futile, the Spirit does not work savingly apart from the Word. The Word is called "the sword of the Spirit" (Eph. 6:17). Again, in II Thessalonians 2:13 we read, "God hath from the beginning chosen you to salvation through sanctification of the Spirit and belief of the truth." There we are told very plainly that even the eternal predestination of God is accomplished by the instrumentality of truth. People are not brought to life whether they know or do not know. They are not given salvation whether they believe the truth or not. On the contrary, God chose them to salvation through "belief of the truth."

The Scripture abounds in so many passages which indicate this same truth that it seems to be laboring the matter unduly to add any further discussion of this emphatic point of the Bible. We may safely conclude that though men may know the truth and not be saved, they cannot be saved except they know the truth.

My dear laymen, laymen must be theologians. No, they need not be professional theologians. They need not study Greek and Hebrew. They need not necessarily be able to teach other people. But they must be theologians. That is, they must know God. They must have sound knowledge about God. They may not excuse themselves from having clear and correct opinions about the Deity on the ground that they are not ordained to full-time church work but have been called to some other service.

The duty to be theologians is common to all of us. The difference at this point between laymen and ministers is a difference not of kind but of degree. It is an error of Rome which teaches that there is a difference of kind between priests and people. With the Bible, the Protestant church teaches that the Bible itself was given not solely to the clergy but to all the people of God. We of the clergy have greater obligation, not sole obligation. So far as time permits, and to the degree that your obligations to this world allow, in that measure must you be familiar with the truth of God. For that knowledge God will hold you responsible in the day of judgment. While you need not read this book or any other particular book except the Book, the Word of God itself, I hope you will read this book to help you in your study of the Bible and in your gaining a sound knowledge of God. But I remind you that while this book may give you some knowledge of God by means of which you may be saved, neither this book nor any other book (not even the Bible itself) can save you. This truth of God must be loved, must be embraced, and must be yielded to if the person who has saving knowledge is to be saved by it. One theologian has written that it is not enough to "understand" but you must also "stand under." For the truth of God is a person—a person who said, "I am the way, the truth, and the life" (John 14:6). A true theologian, therefore, is a person who knows the Person. Everyman must be a theologian.

*Dorothy L. Sayers*

# 4

# Creed or Chaos?

*And when he is come, he will convict the world of sin, and of righteousness, and of judgment: of sin, because they believe not on me; of righteousness, because I go to the Father, and ye see me no more; of judgment, because the prince of this world is judged John 16:8–11.*

Something is happening to us today which has not happened for a very long time. We are waging a war of religion. Not a civil war between adherents of the same religion, but a life-and-death struggle between Christian and pagan. The Christians are, it must be confessed, not very good Christians, and the pagans do not officially proclaim themselves worshipers of Mahound or even of Odin, but the stark fact remains that Christendom and heathendom stand face to face as they have not done in Europe since the days of Charlemagne. In spite of the various vague references in sermons and public speeches to the War as a "crusade," I think we have scarcely begun to realize the full implications of this. It is a phenomenon of quite extraordinary importance. The people who say it is a war to preserve freedom and justice and faith have gone only halfway to the truth. The real question is what economics and politics are to be used for; whether freedom and justice and faith have any right to be considered at all; at bottom it is a violent and irreconcilable quarrel about the nature of God and the nature of man and the ultimate nature of the universe; it is a war of dogma.

The word *dogma* is unpopular, and that is why I have used it. It is our own distrust of dogma that is handicapping us in the struggle. The immense spiritual strength of our opponents lies precisely in the fact that they have fervently embraced, and hold with fanatical fervor, a dogma which is none the less a dogma for being called an "ideology." We on our side have been trying for several centuries to uphold a particular standard of ethical values which derives from Christian dogma, while gradually dispensing with the very dogma which is the sole rational foundation for those values. The rulers of Germany have seen quite clearly that dogma and ethics are inextricably bound together. Having renounced the dogma, they have renounced the ethics as well—and from their point of view they are perfectly right. They have adopted an entirely different dogma, whose ethical scheme has no value for peace or truth, mercy or justice, faith or freedom; and they see no reason why they should practice a set of virtues incompatible with their dogma.

We have been very slow to understand this. We persist in thinking that Germany "really" believes those things to be right that we believe to be right, and is only very naughty in her behavior. That is a thing we find quite familiar. We often do wrong things, knowing them to be wrong. For a long time we kept on imagining that if we granted certain German demands which seemed fairly reasonable, she would stop being naughty and behave according to our ideas of what was right and proper. We still go on scolding Germany for disregarding the standard of European ethics, as though that standard was something which she still acknowledged. It is only with great difficulty that we can bring ourselves to grasp the fact that there is no failure in Germany to live up to her own standards of right conduct. It is something much more terrifying and tremendous; it is that what we believe to be evil, Germany believes to be good. It is a direct repudiation of the basic Christian dogma on which our Mediterranean civilization, such as it is, is grounded.

I do not want now to discuss the ideology of Germany, nor yet that of Russia which, in rather a different way, is also a repudiation of Christendom. Nor do I want to talk about our own war-aims and peace-aims, and how far we are single-minded about them. All I want to say on this point is that, however deeply we have sinned—and God knows we have done plenty of evil in our time—we have not gone so far as to have altogether lost all claim to stand for Christendom. There is a great difference between believing a thing to be right and not doing it, on the one hand, and, on the other, energetically practicing evil in the firm conviction that it is good. In theological language, the one is mortal sin, which is bad enough; the other is the sin against the Holy Ghost, which is without forgiveness simply and solely because the sinner has not the remotest idea that he is sinning at all. So long as we are aware that we are wicked, we are not corrupt beyond all hope. Our present dissatisfaction with ourselves is a good sign. We have only to be careful that we do not get too disheartened and abashed to do anything about it all.

The only reason why I have mentioned Germany is this: that in the present conflict we have before us, in a visible and physical form which we cannot possibly overlook, the final consequences of a quarrel about dogma. A quarrel of that kind can go on for a very long time beneath the surface, and we can ignore it so long as disagreement about dogma is not translated into physical terms. While there is a superficial consensus of opinion about the ethics of behavior, we can easily persuade ourselves that the underlying dogma is immaterial. We can, as we cheerfully say, "agree to differ." "Never mind about theology," we observe in kindly tones, "if we just go on being brotherly to one another it doesn't matter what we believe about God." We are so accustomed to this idea that we are not perturbed by the man who demands: "If I do not believe in the fatherhood of God, why should I believe in the brotherhood of man?" That, we think, is an interesting point of view, but it is only talk—a subject for quiet after-dinner discussion. But if the man goes on to translate his point of view into action, then, to our horror and surprise, the foundations of society are violently shaken, the crust of morality that looked so solid splits apart, and we see that it was only a thin bridge over an abyss in which two dogmas, incompatible as fire and water, are seething explosively together.

Now in this assembly I may take it for granted that we are generally agreed as to what is good and what is evil. However little we may have lived up to our beliefs, I take it that we are ready, if challenged, to cry, like the paladins in the *Song of Roland:*

> Paiens unt tort e Chrestiens unt dreit
> (Pagans are wrong, Christians are in the right.)

The thing I am here to say to you is this: that it is worse than useless for Christians to talk about the importance of Christian morality, unless they are prepared to take their stand upon the fundamentals of Christian theology. It is a lie to say that dogma does not matter; it matters enormously. It is fatal to let people suppose that Christianity is only a mode of feeling; it is vitally necessary to insist that it is first and foremost a rational explanation of the universe. It is hopeless to offer Christianity as a vaguely idealistic aspiration of a simple and consoling kind; it is, on the contrary, a hard, tough, exacting, and complex doctrine, steeped in a drastic and uncompromising realism. And it is fatal to imagine that everybody knows quite well what Christianity is and needs only a little encouragement to practice it. The brutal fact is that in this Christian country not one person in a hundred has the faintest notion what the church teaches about God or man or society or the person of Jesus Christ. If you think I am exaggerating, ask the Army chaplains. Apart from a possible one percent of intelligent and instructed Christians, there are three kinds of people we have to deal with. There are the frank and open heathen, whose notions of Christianity are a dreadful jumble of rags and tags of Bible anecdote and clotted mythological nonsense. There are the ignorant Christians, who combine a mild gentle-Jesus sentimentality with vaguely humanistic ethics—most of these are Arian heretics. Finally, there are the more or less instructed churchgoers, who know all the arguments about divorce and auricular confession and communion in two kinds, but are about as well equipped to do battle on fundamentals against a Marxian atheist or a Wellsian agnostic as a boy with a peashooter facing a fan-fire of machine guns. Theologically, this country is at present in a state of utter chaos, established in the name of religious toleration, and rapidly degenerating into the flight from reason and the death of hope. We are not happy in this condition, and there are signs of a very great eagerness, especially among the younger people, to find a creed to which they can give wholehearted adherence.

This is the church's opportunity, if she chooses to take it. So far as the people's readiness to listen goes, she has not been in so strong a position for at least two centuries. The rival philosophies of humanism, enlightened self-interest, and mechanical progress have broken down badly; the antagonism of science has proved to be far more apparent than real, and the happy-go-lucky doctrine of *laisser-faire* is completely discredited. But no good whatever will be done by a retreat into personal piety or by mere exhortation to a "recall to prayer." The thing that is in danger is the whole structure of society, and it is necessary to persuade thinking men and women of the vital and intimate connection between the structure of society and the theological doctrines of Christianity.

The task is not made easier by the obstinate refusal of a great body of nominal Christians, both lay and clerical, to face the theological question. "Take away theology and give us some nice religion" has been a popular slogan for so long that we are apt to accept it, without inquiring whether religion without theology has any meaning. And however unpopular I may make myself, I shall and will affirm that the reason why the churches are discredited today is not that they are too bigoted about theology, but that they have run away from theology. The Church of Rome alone has retained her prestige because she puts theology in the foreground of her teaching. Some of us may perhaps think it a rather unimaginative and confined theology; but that is not the point. The point is that the Church of Rome is a theological society, in a sense in which the Church of England, taken as a whole, is not, and that because of this insistence on theology, she is a body disciplined, honored, and sociologically important.

I should like to do two things this afternoon. First, to point out that if we really want a Christian society we must teach Christianity, and that it is absolutely impossible to teach Christianity without teaching Christian dogma. Secondly, to put before you a list of half a dozen or so main doctrinal points which the world most especially needs to have drummed into its ears at this moment—doctrines forgotten or misinterpreted, but which (if they are true as the church maintains them to be) are cornerstones in that rational structure of human society which is the alternative to world-chaos.

I will begin with this matter of the inevitability of dogma, if Christianity is to be anything more than a little mild wishful thinking about ethical behavior.

Writing the other day in *The Spectator,* Dr. Selbie, former principal of Mansfield College, discussed the subject of "The Army and the Churches." In the course of this article there occurs a passage that exposes the root-cause of the failure of the churches to influence the life of the common people.

> ... the rise of the new dogmatism (he says) whether in its Calvinist or Thomist form, constitutes a fresh and serious threat to Christian unity. The tragedy is that *all this, however interesting to theologians, is hopelessly irrelevant to the life and thought of the average man,* who is more puzzled than ever by the disunion of the Churches, and by the theological and ecclesiastical differences on which it is based.

Now I am perfectly ready to agree that disputes between

the churches constitute a menace to Christendom. And I will admit that I am not quite sure what is meant by "the new dogmatism"; it might, I suppose, mean the appearance of new dogmas among the followers of St. Thomas and Calvin respectively. But I rather fancy it means, a fresh attention to, and reassertion of, old dogma, and that when Dr. Selbie says that "all this" is irrelevant to the life and thought of the average man, he is deliberately saying that Christian dogma, as such, is irrelevant.

But if Christian dogma is irrelevant to life, to what, in heaven's name is it relevant?—since religious dogma is in fact nothing but a statement of doctrines concerning the nature of life and the universe. If Christian ministers really believe it is only an intellectual game for theologians and has no bearing upon human life, it is no wonder that their congregations are ignorant, bored, and bewildered. And indeed, in the very next paragraph, Dr. Selbie recognizes the relation of Christian dogma to life:

> . . . peace can only come about through a practical application of Christian principles and values. But this must have behind it *something more than a reaction against* that *Pagan Humanism* which has now been found wanting.

The "something else" is dogma, and cannot be anything else, for between humanism and Christianity and between paganism and theism there is no distinction whatever except a distinction of dogma. That you cannot have Christian principles without Christ is becoming increasingly clear, because their validity as principles depends on Christ's authority; and as we have seen, the totalitarian states, having ceased to believe in Christ's authority, are logically quite justified in repudiating Christian principles. If "the average man" is required to "believe in Christ" and accept His authority for "Christian principles," it is surely relevant to inquire who or what Christ is, and why His authority should be accepted. But the question, "What think ye of Christ?" lands the average man at once in the very knottiest kind of dogmatic riddle. It is quite useless to say that it doesn't matter particularly who or what Christ was or by what authority He did those things, and that even if He was only a man, He was a very nice man and we ought to live by His principles: for that is merely humanism, and if the "average man" in Germany chooses to think that Hitler is a nicer sort of man with still more attractive principles, the Christian humanist has no answer to make.

It is not true at all that dogma is "hopelessly irrelevant" to the life and thought of the average man. What is true is that ministers of the Christian religion often assert that it is, present it for consideration as though it were, and, in fact, by their faulty exposition of it make it so. The central dogma of the incarnation is that by which relevance stands or falls. If Christ was only man, if He is only God, then He is entirely irrelevant to any experience of human life. It is, in the strictest sense, *necessary* to the salvation of relevance that a man should believe *rightly* the incarnation of our Lord Jesus Christ. Unless he believes rightly, there is not the faintest reason why he should believe at all. And in that case, it is wholly irrelevant to chatter about "Christian principles."

If the "average man" is going to be interested in Christ at all, it is the dogma that will provide the interest. The trouble is that, in nine cases out of ten, he has never been offered the dogma. What he has been offered is a set of technical theological terms which nobody has taken the trouble to translate into language relevant to ordinary life.

"... Jesus Christ, the Son of God, is God and man." What does this suggest, except that God the Creator (the irritable old gentleman with the beard) in some mysterious manner fathered upon the Virgin Mary something amphibious, neither one thing nor t'other, like a merman? And, like human sons, wholly distinct from and (with some excuse) probably antagonistic to the father? And what, in any case, has this remarkable hybrid to do with John Brown or Tommy Atkins? This attitude of mind is that called by theologians Nestorianism, or perhaps a debased form of Arianism. But we really cannot just give it a technical label and brush it aside as something irrelevant to the thought of the average man. The average man produced it. It is, in fact, an immediate and unsophisticated expression of the thought of the average man. And at the risk of plunging him into the abominable heresy of the Patripassians or the Theo-Paschites, we must unite with Athanasius to assure Tommy Atkins that the God who lived and died in the world was the same God who made the world, and that, therefore, God Himself has the best possible reasons for understanding and sympathizing with Tommy's personal troubles.

"But," Tommy Atkins and John Brown will instantly object, "it can't have mattered very much to Him if He was God. A god can't really suffer like you and me. Besides, the parson says we are to try and be like Christ; but that's all nonsense—we can't be God, and it's silly to ask us to try." This able exposition of the Eutychian heresy can scarcely be dismissed as merely "interesting to theologians"; it appears to interest Atkins and Brown to the point of irritation. Willy-nilly, we are forced to involve ourselves further in dogmatic theology and insist that Christ is "perfect God *and perfect man.*"

At this point, language will trip us up. The average man is not to be restrained from thinking that "perfect God" implies a comparison with gods less perfect, and that "perfect man" means "the best kind of man you can possibly have." While both these propositions are quite true, they are not precisely what we want to convey. It will perhaps be better to say, "altogether God and altogether man"—God and man at the same time, in every respect and completely; God from eternity to eternity and from the womb to the grave, a man also from the womb to the grave and now.

"That," replies Tommy Atkins, "is all very well, but it leaves me cold. Because, if He was God all the time He must have known that His sufferings and death and so on wouldn't last, and He could have stopped them by a miracle if He had liked, so His pretending to be an ordinary man was nothing but play-acting." And John Brown adds, "You can't call a person 'altogether man' if He was God and didn't *want* to do anything wrong. It was easy enough for Him to be good, but it's not at all the same thing for me. How about all that temptation stuff? Play-acting again. It doesn't help *me* to live what you call a Christian life."

John and Tommy are now on the way to become convinced Apollinarians, a fact which, however "interesting to theologians," has a distinct relevance also to the lives of those average men, since they propose, on the strength of it, to dismiss "Christian principles" as impracticable. There is no help for it. We must insist upon Christ's possession of "a reasonable soul" as well as "human flesh"; we must admit the human limitations of knowledge and intellect; we must take a hint from Christ Himself and suggest that miracles belong to the Son of Man as well as to the Son of God; we must postulate a human will liable to temptation; and we must be equally firm about "Equal to the Father as touching His Godhead *and inferior to the Father as touching His manhood.*" Complicated as the theology is, the average man has walked straight into the heart of the Athanasian Creed, and we are bound to follow.

Teachers and preachers never, I think, make it sufficiently clear that dogmas are not a set of arbitrary regulations invented *a priori* by a committee of theologians enjoying a bout of all-in dialectical wrestling. Most of them were hammered out under pressure of urgent practical necessity to provide an answer to heresy. And heresy is, as I have tried to show, largely the expression of opinion of the untutored average man, trying to grapple with the problems of the universe at the point where they begin to interfere with his daily life and thought. To me, engaged in my diabolical occupation of going to and fro in the world and walking up and down in it, conversations and correspondence bring daily a magnificent crop of all the standard heresies. As practical examples of the "life and

thought of the average man," I am extremely well familiar
with them, though I had to hunt through the encyclopedia
to fit them with their proper theological titles for the purposes of this address. For the answers I need not go so far:
they are compendiously set forth in the creeds. But an
interesting fact is this: that nine out of ten of my heretics
are exceedingly surprised to discover that the creeds contain any statements that bear a practical and comprehensible meaning. If I tell them it is an article of faith that the
same God who made the world endured the suffering of
the world, they ask in perfect good faith what connection
there is between that statement and the story of Jesus. If I
draw their attention to the dogma that the same Jesus who
was the Divine Love was also Light of Light, the Divine
Wisdom, they are surprised. Some of them thank me very
heartily for this entirely novel and original interpretation
of Scripture, which they never heard of before and suppose me to have invented. Others say irritably that they
don't like to think that wisdom and religion have anything
to do with one another, and that I should do much better
to cut out the wisdom and reason and intelligence and stick
to a simple gospel of love. But whether they are pleased or
annoyed, they are interested; and the thing that interests
them, whether or not they suppose it to be my invention, is
the resolute assertion of the dogma.

As regards Dr. Selbie's complaint that insistence on
dogma only affronts people and throws into relief the in-
ternecine quarrels of Christendom, may I say two things?
First, I believe it to be a grave mistake to present Christianity as something charming and popular with no offense in it. Seeing that Christ went about the world giving
the most violent offense to all kinds of people, it would
seem absurd to expect that the doctrine of His Person can
be so presented as to offend nobody. We cannot blink the
fact that gentle Jesus meek and mild was so stiff in His
opinions and so inflammatory in His language that He was
thrown out of church, stoned, hunted from place to place,
and finally gibbeted as a firebrand and a public danger.

Whatever His peace was, it was not the peace of an amiable indifference; and He said in so many words that what He brought with Him was fire and sword. That being so, nobody need be too much surprised or disconcerted at finding that a determined preaching of Christian dogma may sometimes result in a few angry letters of protest or a difference of opinion on the parish council.

The other thing is this: that I find by experience there is a very large measure of agreement among Christian denominations on all doctrine that is really ecumenical. A rigidly Catholic interpretation of the creeds, for example—including the Athanasian Creed—will find support both in Rome and in Geneva. Objections will come chiefly from the heathen, and from a noisy but not very representative bunch of heretical parsons who once in their youth read Robertson or Conybeare and have never got over it. But what is urgently necessary is that certain fundamentals should be restated in terms that make their meaning—and indeed, the mere fact that they *have* a meaning—clear to the ordinary uninstructed heathen to whom technical theological language has become a dead letter.

May I now mention some of the dogmas concerning which I find there is most ignorance and misunderstanding and about which I believe the modern world most urgently needs to be told? Out of a very considerable number I have selected seven as being what I may call "key positions," namely, God, man, sin, judgment, matter, work, and society. They are, of course, all closely bound together—Christian doctrine is not a set of rules, but one vast interlocking rational structure—but there are particular aspects of these seven subjects which seem to me to need special emphasis at the moment.

1. **God.** At the risk of appearing quite insolently obvious, I shall say that if the church is to make any impression on the modern mind she will have to preach Christ and the cross.

Of late years, the church has not succeeded very well in

preaching Christ: she has preached Jesus, which is not quite the same thing. I find that the ordinary man simply does not grasp *at all* the idea that Jesus Christ and God the Creator are held to be literally the same person. They believe Catholic doctrine to be that God the Father made the world and that Jesus Christ redeemed mankind, and that these two characters are quite separate personalities. The phrasing of the Nicene Creed is here a little unfortunate—it is easy to read it as: "being of one substance with the-Father-by-whom-all-things-were-made." The church catechism—again rather unfortunately—emphasizes the distinction: "God the Father who hath made me and all the world, God the Son who hath redeemed me and all mankind." The distinction of the persons within unity of the substance is philosophically quite proper, and familiar enough to any creative artist: but the majority of people are not creative artists, and they have it very firmly fixed in their heads that the person who bore the sins of the world was not the eternal creative life of the world, but an entirely different person, who was in fact the victim of God the Creator. It is dangerous to emphasize one aspect of a doctrine at the expense of the other, but at this present moment the danger that anybody will confound the persons is so remote as to be negligible. What everybody does is to divide the substance—with the result that the whole Jesus-history becomes an unmeaning anecdote of the brutality of God to man.

It is only with the confident assertion of the creative divinity of the Son that the doctrine of the incarnation becomes a real revelation of the structure of the world. And here Christianity has its enormous advantage over every other religion in the world. It is the *only* religion which gives value to evil and suffering. It affirms—not, like Christian Science, that evil has no real existence, nor yet, like Buddhism, that good consists in a refusal to experience evil—but that perfection is attained through the active and positive effort to wrench a real good out of a real evil.

I will not now go into the very difficult question of the nature of evil and the reality of not-being, though the modern physicists seem to be giving us a very valuable lead about that particular philosophic dilemma. But it seems to me most important that, in face of present world conditions, the doctrines of the reality of evil and the value of suffering should be kept in the very front line of Christian affirmation. I mean, it is not enough to say that religion produces virtues and personal consolations side by side with the very obvious evils and pains that afflict mankind, but that God is alive and at work *within* the evil and the suffering, perpetually transforming them by the positive energy which He had with the Father before the world was made.

2. **Man.** A young and intelligent priest remarked to me the other day that he thought one of the greatest sources of strength in Christianity today lay in the profoundly pessimistic view it took of human nature. There is a great deal in what he says. The people who are most discouraged and made despondent by the barbarity and stupidity of human behavior at this time are those who think highly of *Homo Sapiens* as a product of evolution, and who still cling to an optimistic belief in the civilizing influence of progress and enlightenment. To them, the appalling outbursts of bestial ferocity in the totalitarian states, and the obstinate selfishness and stupid greed of capitalist society, are not merely shocking and alarming. For them, these things are the utter negation of everything in which they have believed. It is as though the bottom had dropped out of their universe. The whole thing looks like a denial of all reason, and they feel as if they and the world had gone mad together. Now for the Christian, this is not so. He is as deeply shocked and grieved as anybody else, but he is not astonished. He has never thought very highly of human nature left to itself. He has been accustomed to the idea that there is a deep interior dislocation in the very center of human personality, and that you can never, as they say, "make people good by Act of Parliament," just because

laws are man-made and therefore partake of the imperfect and self-contradictory nature of man. Humanly speaking, it is not true at all that "truly to know the good is to do the good"; it is far truer to say with St. Paul that "the evil that I would not, that I do"; so that the mere increase of knowledge is of very little help in the struggle to outlaw evil. The delusion of the mechanical perfectibility of mankind through a combined process of scientific knowledge and unconscious evolution has been responsible for a great deal of heartbreak. It is, at bottom, far more pessimistic than Christian pessimism, because, if science and progress break down, there is nothing to fall back upon. Humanism is self-contained—it provides for man no resources outside himself. The Christian dogma of the double nature in man—which asserts that man is disintegrated and necessarily imperfect in himself and all his works, yet closely related by a real unity of substance with an eternal perfection within and beyond him—makes the present parlous state of human society seem both less hopeless and less irrational. I say "the present parlous state"—but that is to limit it too much. A man told me the other day: "I have a little boy of a year old. When the war broke out, I was very much distressed about him, because I found I was taking it for granted that life *ought* to be better and easier for him than it had been for my generation. Then I realized that I had no right to take this for granted at all—that the fight between good and evil must be the same for him as it had always been, and then I ceased to feel so much distressed." As Lord David Cecil has said: "The jargon of the philosophy of progress taught us to think that the savage and primitive state of man is behind us; we still talk of the present 'return to barbarism.' But barbarism is not behind us, it is beneath us." And in the same article he observes: "Christianity has compelled the mind of man, not because it is the most cheering view of human existence, but because it is truest to the facts." I think this is true; and it seems to me quite disastrous that the idea should have got about that Christianity is an other-worldly, unreal, idealistic kind of religion which suggests that if we are good we shall be happy—or if not, it will all be made up to us in the next existence. On the contrary, it is fiercely and even harshly realistic, insisting that the kingdom of heaven can never be attained in this world except by unceasing toil and struggle and vigilance: that, in fact, we cannot be good and cannot be happy, but that there are certain eternal achievements that make even happiness look like trash. It has been said, I think by Berdyaev, that nothing can prevent the human soul from preferring creativeness to happiness. In this lies man's substantial likeness to the divine Christ who in this world suffers and creates continually, being incarnate in the bonds of matter.

3. **Sin.** This doctrine of man leads naturally to the doctrine of sin. One of the really surprising things about the present bewilderment of humanity is that the Christian church now finds herself called upon to proclaim the old and hated doctrine of sin as a gospel of cheer and encouragement. The final tendency of the modern philosophies—hailed in their day as a release from the burden of sinfulness—has been to bind man hard and fast in the chains of an iron determinism. The influences of heredity and environment, of glandular make-up and the control exercised by the unconscious, of economic necessity and the mechanics of biological development, have all been invoked to assure man that he is not responsible for his misfortunes and therefore not to be held guilty. Evil has been represented as something imposed upon him from without, not made by him from within. The dreadful conclusion follows inevitably, that as he is not responsible for evil, he cannot alter it; even though evolution and progress may offer some alleviation in the future, there is no hope for you and me, here and now. I well remember how an aunt of mine, brought up in an old-fashioned liberalism, protested angrily against having continually to call herself a "miserable sinner" when reciting the litany. Today, if we could really be persuaded that we *are* miserable sinners—that the trouble is not outside us but inside us,

and that therefore, by the grace of God we can do something to put it right, we should receive that message as the most hopeful and heartening thing that can be imagined.

Needless to say, the whole doctrine of "original sin" will have to be restated, in terms which the ordinary modern man, brought up on biology and Freudian psychology, can understand. These sciences have done an enormous amount to expose the *nature* and *mechanism* of man's inner dislocation and ought to be powerful weapons in the hand of the church. It is a thousand pities that the church should ever have allowed these weapons to be turned against her.

4. **Judgment.** Much the same thing is true of the doctrine of judgment. The word *punishment* for sin has become so corrupted that it ought never to be used. But once we have established the true doctrine of man's nature, the true nature of judgment becomes startlingly clear and rational. It is the inevitable consequence of man's attempt to regulate life and society on a system that runs counter to the facts of his own nature. In the physical sphere, typhus and cholera are a judgment on dirty living; not because God shows an arbitrary favoritism to nice, clean people, but because of an essential element in the physical structure of the universe. In the state, the brutal denial of freedom to the individual will issue in a judgment of blood, because man is so made that oppression is more intolerable to him than death. The avaricious greed that prompts men to cut down forests for the speedy making of money brings down a judgment of flood and famine, because that sin of avarice in the spiritual sphere runs counter to the physical law of nature. We must not say that such behavior is wrong because it does not pay; but rather that it does not pay because it is wrong. As T. S. Eliot says: "A wrong attitude towards nature implies, somewhere, a wrong attitude towards God, and the consequence is an inevitable doom."

5. **Matter.** At this point we shall find ourselves compelled to lay down the Christian doctrine concerning the material universe; and it is here, I think, that we shall have

our best opportunity to explain the meaning of sacramentalism. The common man labors under a delusion that for the Christian, matter is evil and the body is evil. For this misapprehension, St. Paul must bear some blame, St. Augustine of Hippo a good deal more, and Calvin a very great deal. But so long as the church continues to teach the manhood of God and to celebrate the sacraments of the Eucharist and of marriage, no living man should dare to say that matter and body are not sacred to her. She must insist strongly that the whole material universe is an expression and incarnation of the creative energy of God, as a book or a picture is the material expression of the creative soul of the artist. For that reason, all good and creative handling of the material universe is holy and beautiful, and all abuse of the material universe is a crucifixion of the body of Christ. The whole question of the right use to be made of art, of the intellect, and of the material resources of the world is bound up in this. Because of this, the exploitation of man or of matter for commercial uses stands condemned, together with all debasement of the arts and perversions of the intellect. If matter and the physical nature of man are evil, or if they are of no importance except as they serve an economic system, then there is nothing to restrain us from abusing them as we choose—nothing, except the absolute certainty that any such abuse will eventually come up against the unalterable law and issue in judgment and destruction. In these as in all other matters we cannot escape the law; we have only the choice of fulfilling it freely by the way of grace or willy-nilly by the way of judgment.

6. **Work.** The unsacramental attitude of modern society to man and matter is probably closely connected with its unsacramental attitude to work. The church is a good deal to blame for having connived at this. From the eighteenth century onwards, she has tended to acquiesce in what I may call the "industrious apprentice" view of the matter: "Work hard and be thrifty, and God will bless you with a contented mind and a competence." This is nothing but

enlightened self-interest in its vulgarest form, and plays directly into the hands of the monopolist and the financier. Nothing has so deeply discredited the Christian church as her squalid submission to the economic theory of society. The burning question of the Christian attitude to money is being so eagerly debated nowadays that it is scarcely necessary to do more than remind ourselves that the present unrest, both in Russia and in Central Europe, is an immediate judgment upon a financial system that has subordinated man to economics, and that no *mere* readjustment of economic machinery will have any lasting effect if it keeps man a prisoner inside the machine.

This is the burning question; but I believe there is a still more important and fundamental question waiting to be dealt with, and that is, what men in a Christian society ought to think and feel about work. Curiously enough, apart from the passage in Genesis which suggests that work is a hardship and a judgment on sin, Christian doctrine is not very explicit about work. I believe, however, that there *is* a Christian doctrine of work, very closely related to the doctrines of the creative energy of God and the divine image in man. The modern tendency seems to be to identify work with gainful employment; and this is, I maintain, the essential heresy at the back of the great economic fallacy which allows wheat and coffee to be burnt and fish to be used for manure while whole populations stand in need of food. The fallacy being that work is not the expression of man's creative energy in the service of society, but only something he does in order to obtain money and leisure.

A very able surgeon put it to me like this: "What is happening," he said, "is that nobody works for the sake of getting the thing done. The result of the work is a by-product; the *aim* of the work is to make money to do something else. Doctors practice medicine, not primarily to relieve suffering, but to make a living—the cure of the patient is something that happens on the way. Lawyers accept briefs, not because they have a passion for justice, but because the law is the profession which enables them to live. The reason," he added, "why men often find themselves happy and satisfied in the army is that for the first time in their lives they find themselves doing something, not for the sake of the pay, which is miserable, but for the sake of getting the thing done."

I will only add to this one thing which seems to me very symptomatic. I was shown a "scheme for a Christian Society" drawn up by a number of young and earnest Roman Catholics. It contained a number of clauses dealing with work and employment—minimum wages, hours of labor, treatment of employees, housing, and so on—all very proper and Christian. But it offered no machinery whatever for ensuring that the work itself should be properly done. In its lack of a sacramental attitude to work, that is, it was as empty as a set of trade union regulations. We may remember that a medieval guild did insist, not only on the employer's duty to his workmen, but also on the laborer's duty to his work.

If man's fulfillment of his nature is to be found in the full expression of his divine creativeness, then we urgently need a Christian doctrine of work, which shall provide, not only for proper conditions of employment, but also that the work shall be such as a man may do with his whole heart, and that he shall do it for the very work's sake. But we cannot expect a sacramental attitude to work, while many people are forced, by our evil standard of values, to do work which is a spiritual degradation—a long series of financial trickeries, for example, or the manufacture of vulgar and useless trivialities.

7. **Society.** Lastly, a word or two about the Christian doctrine of society—not about its translation into political terms, but about its dogmatic basis. It rests on the doctrine of what God is and what man *is,* and it is impossible to have a Christian doctrine of society *except* as a corollary to Christian dogma about the place of man in the universe. This is, or should be, obvious. The one point to which I should like to draw attention is the Christian doctrine of

the moral law. The attempt to abolish wars and wickedness by the moral law is doomed to failure, because of the fact of sinfulness. Law, like every other product of human activity, shares the integral human imperfection: it is, in the old Calvinistic phrase: "of the nature of sin." That is to say: all legality, if erected into an absolute value, contains within itself the seeds of judgment and catastrophe. The law is necessary, but only, as it were, as a protective fence against the forces of evil, behind which the divine activity of grace may do its redeeming work. We can, for example, never make a positive peace or a positive righteousness by enactments against offenders; law is always prohibitive, negative, and corrupted by the interior contradictions of man's divided nature; it belongs to the category of judgment. That is why an intelligent understanding about sin is necessary to preserve the world from putting an unjustified confidence in the efficacy of the moral law taken by itself. It will never drive out Beelzebub; it cannot, because it is only human and not divine.

Nevertheless, the law must be rightly understood or it is not possible to make the world understand the meaning of grace. There is only one real law—the law of the universe; it may be fulfilled either by way of judgment or by the way of grace, but it *must* be fulfilled one way or the other. If men will not understand the meaning of judgment, they will never come to understand the meaning of grace. If they hear not Moses or the prophets, neither will they be persuaded, though one rose from the dead.

An address delivered at Derby, England, May 4, 1940. Reprinted with permission of A. Watkins, Inc., from *Creed or Chaos?* by Dorothy L. Sayers. Copyright 1949 by Dorothy L. Sayers.

*Kenneth F. W. Prior*

# 5

# The Minister
# As Teacher

A suitable text to write over this chapter is Proverbs 4:13: "Take fast hold of instruction; let her not go; keep her; for she is thy life." These words indicate the importance of teaching and instruction in the Christian life, and therefore the place that they ought to occupy in the Christian ministry. Today we need men and women with a firm grip on vital truths, who can stand on their own feet amidst all the pressures of present-day life. Church members need to be not just "babes in Christ" but mature, adult believers who can give "a reason for the hope that is within them." Our opening words from Proverbs suggest that it is all too easy to fall short here, and that considerable effort is involved in maintaining it. So we should not be surprised that teaching calls for considerable diligence on the part of the minister and effort on the part of the hearer.

## The Importance of the Teaching Ministry

First of all, let us notice that the teaching ministry is demanded by the *very nature of biblical truth itself*. After all, the Bible is full of instruction on both doctrinal and practical matters, and this teaching is intended for the rank-and-file members of the church. The Bible was written not just for theologians but was addressed to all of God's people. When Paul wrote his Epistles, for example, he was not addressing theological experts, but ordinary members of the church. Let us also remember that the New Testament apostles were fully aware of the limitations of their hearers. The same apostle who wrote the Epistle to the Romans, with all its deep, doctrinal teaching, was also aware that the churches of his day included "not many wise men after the flesh, not many mighty, not many noble" (I Cor. 1:26). This means that a minister of the Word of God, whatever the congregation with which he is faced, whether it be rich or poor, educated or uneducated, must teach. He may well of course adjust his method to fit in with the need and capabilities of those before him, but he still cannot evade his responsibility to teach the truth of God to those committed to his charge. Indeed, is not every minister in the Church of England asked at his ordination, "Are you determined, out of the said Scriptures, to instruct the people committed to your charge?"

*Teaching is also demanded by the needs of Christians.* Here is the way of stability. Peter speaks of those who are "unlearned and unstable" (II Peter 3:16); how often these two deficiencies go together! Thomas Watson in the *Body of Divinity* quotes this verse and continues: "Such as are unlearned in the main points of divinity are unstable. As the body cannot be strong that has the sinews shrunk; so neither can the Christian be strong in religion who wants the grounds of knowledge, which are the sinews to strengthen and establish him." Here is where the work of pastor and teacher is so necessary, and is one of the important functions that the ascended Christ has delegated to His ministers. The purpose is to produce a maturity among God's people which is demonstrated by their stability, as Paul tells us, ". . . unto the measure of the stature of the fulness of Christ; that we henceforth be no more children, tossed to and fro, and carried about with every wind of doctrine" (see Eph. 4:11–14).

I have often discovered this in experience. What the unstable Christian needs is not repeated acts of consecration, but simply to be taught. The trouble is he is not sure of himself, and doctrine can be like a backbone in an otherwise flabby Christian. I have often talked to those who were brought up in evangelical circles in the earlier years of this century and have since fallen away. Again and again they have described their departure from evangelical ways as "growing out of it." Does this indicate that the teaching they received never graduated past the Sunday school lesson and was inadequate for the demands of adult life? I suspect that young people whose spiritual lives simply revolve around a Saturday night interdenominational rally, where their spiritual diet gets little beyond the singing of spiritual nursery rhymes, have great problems in standing for Christ in the world, unless they withdraw themselves and live a sheltered life.

We ought also to bear in mind that soundness in doctrine is essential to spiritual health. In II Peter 2:1 we read of "damnable heresies," and it is good for us to remember the warning of Thomas Watson, "A man may go to hell as well for heresy as for adultery." This does not mean that we anathematize those who do not agree with us in all points of doctrine; nor is it an excuse for heresy-hunting. Nevertheless, there are *basic doctrines* which are vital to our spiritual well-being.

A third way in which teaching is demanded is by *the pressures from outside.* In the world we are surrounded by intellectual agnosticism, and our young people in these days have a great deal to stand against. Let us remember that the reason, very frequently, for feeble witness on the part of a young Christian is simply the awareness that he doesn't know his stuff, and that he can be bowled over by any self-confident agnostic.

There are pressures, too, in the rest of the church. Evangelicals in these days face many problems. What is the answer? To shut our eyes to these pressures and to stick to the "simple gospel" may well be suicide. The great need, surely, is for our people to be taught the vital, evangelical truths of Holy Scripture. When we are in a position of strength, then we are not afraid to get involved in ecumenical discussions. Paul's answer to the legalistic ritualism of his day was the Epistle to the Galatians, and his reply to Gnostic philosophy was the Epistle to the Colossians. We need to do the same. On our committees we need men of understanding who can distinguish between truth and error. When evangelistic campaigns are organized we need evangelical laymen, who are not just carried away by oratory or commanding personalities when assessing evangelists, but can recognize those who appeal for decisions on only a quarter of the gospel!

A great deal is made amongst evangelicals in these days of the importance of lay ministry; indeed, for many years laymen have been very useful in speaking at young people's meetings and so on. However, if laymen are to be used in this way, they need to be taught before they can be expected to teach others. Let us remember that just because a man is well known in a secular occupation, and in consequence may well draw a crowd when he speaks at a meeting, this does not necessarily mean he is qualified to unfold the things of God.

## How Are Men to Be Taught?

One obvious answer is for them to teach themselves, and in this do-it-yourself age this is sure to commend itself to many. Undoubtedly, this has often happened, and it is good to have in our congregations men who are prepared to read and study. Here surely is the value of a church bookstall, and why we should encourage our church members to read. Supremely, of course, we encourage Christians to undertake personal Bible study and are ready to commend well-tried methods.

However, much as we recognize the importance of the foregoing, Scripture lays the greatest emphasis on the teaching ministry. In the pastoral Epistles, Paul lays before Timothy the need to find "faithful men, who shall be able to teach others also" (II Tim. 2:2). Dr. J. I. Packer has surely spotted this emphasis when he writes, "There is something deeply unnatural and unsatisfactory in a situation where the people of God have to rely entirely on personal Bible study for their spiritual nourishment, due to lack of effective expository preaching in public worship." And again, "The New Testament pattern is that public preaching of God's Word provides, so to speak, the main meals, and constitutes the chief means of grace, and one's own meditations on biblical truth should come in as ancillary to this, having the nature of a series of supplementary snacks—necessary indeed in their place, but never intended to stand alone as a complete diet" (*God Has Spoken,* p. 91).

Notice that Dr. Packer in the above quotation speaks of "effective expository preaching in public worship." I am quite sure that this is the place where a teaching ministry should be exercised, *i.e.* in the pulpit on Sundays. I believe this should take precedence over midweek meetings, and if shortage of time is a problem, I don't think there is any doubt about where the priority should lie. We need to compare the time we spend in preparation for a small gathering in the week, with that for the larger numbers on Sunday. I also wonder whether some clergy make the mistake of trying to give too many addresses and, as a result, their quality suffers.

At the same time, there is surely a place for basic instruction regularly given. An obvious example of this is found in confirmation classes, which I have always combined with a class for new converts and enquirers. I have also given a two-year cycle of Christian doctrine lectures covering the whole range of Christian doctrine. This seems to be the best way of teaching people some of the basic matters of the Christian faith, rather than leaving them to pick up ideas here and there from sermons and talks that they hear. Of course this fits in very well with a moving population, many of whom tend to be members of the church for about two years. I see no reason, however, why the same kind of thing should not be done in any parish, where instead of a moving population there is a growing-up one. What a help it is if all of our young people as they emerge from our youth organization have a thorough grounding in Christian doctrine and know the difference between truth and error, and between the right and wrong. Also, once a cycle of instruction has been prepared, it can be used several times with little further work. And why shouldn't painstaking preparation be put to the greatest possible use?

## The Demands of the Teaching Ministry

There is no doubt that a teaching ministry makes great demands on the one who gives it. His supreme need is surely for the special gift of the Holy Spirit for this purpose. Let us remember that the ability to teach the truths of God is not necessarily an academic one. There are men with first-class theological degrees who are good teachers, and others with the same qualifications who don't even know where to begin. At the same time, there are those without such specialist training who have great ability in delivering the truth of God to an ordinary congregation. It is worth noticing the prominent place that the gift of teaching is given amongst the gifts of the Spirit in I Corinthians 12. If we regard the work of apostles and prophets as applying especially to the age in which the New Testament was still being written, then the gift of teaching comes first on the list that remains. Paul tells us to seek earnestly the best gifts, and if God calls a man to stand in a pulpit most Sundays of the year, we might expect this to be the very gift that God will give him.

An essential part of the equipment for a teaching ministry is, of course, the minister's library. He needs commentaries and doctrinal works if he is to fulfill the promise at his ordination to be diligent in his study of Holy Scripture. He will also learn all he can from books written by those who know how to communicate to the kind of people with whom he is concerned. He will also need to keep abreast of what is happening in the world and the way that people are thinking. A good newspaper is a help here.

Another need for the teaching ministry is that it should be combined with that of the pastor. Is it an accident that pastors and teachers are mentioned together in Ephesians 4? I think not. If we are to be effective in our teaching it is no use simply being men of the library. If we are to bring the truth of God to bear upon people we must be in touch with them. A church warden from a church that was re-nowned for its teaching ministry once complained to me that the sermons they heard were little more than a theological exercise, and the one who gave them was so utterly harsh and unsympathetic towards his hearers. I remember also hearing of a vicar who gave a series of sermons on problems that people raise, only to discover after a while that the problems on which he was preaching were nobody else's but his own. The New Testament apos-tles were in close touch with people and their problems and failures. Professor James Stewart said of Paul in *A Man in Christ*, "Paul's religious position was hammered out, not in the study, but on the mission field."

Then there is the need for time, for there is no doubt that preparation for a teaching ministry is time-consuming, and there are no shortcuts for this. We have to remember that we need time not only for the preparation of next Sunday's sermons, but also for reading and study to lay in store for the future. The principle of sowing and reaping applies here: if we fail in our reading and study, we feel the lack of it a year or two later. Most of us find that the greatest demand of preaching arises from it having to be maintained week after week and year after year.

There is only one way to keep fresh, unless of course we move from one church to another every two years—and it has not been unknown for clergy to resort to this!

Now the Bible clearly recognizes this need for time. In Acts 6 we have the well-known occasion when the apostles saw the need to be set free from administration so that they could give themselves "continually to prayer, and the ministry of the Word" (here is another significant combination!).

We are here confronted with a familiar problem: it is often a great struggle to get all the time that we need. Many churches do not help as much as they could in this matter. Some church members have no idea of the time needed for preparation. A regular churchgoer once expressed surprise on discovering that I needed to prepare sermons. She thought that all my studying had been completed in theological college and that I now made up my sermons as I preached them! I must say I was taken aback that my sermons had left her with this impression. Of course some clergy have only themselves to blame and seem to think it is part of their ministry to spend a lot of time organizing stunts, collecting articles for sales, attending social functions, and so on. Sometimes it is sheer indiscipline that robs us of much of our time. Most of us find that getting time for adequate preparation is a struggle, but we must never give up.

### The Method of the Teaching Ministry

Surely the method for a teaching ministry should be expository preaching. This means nothing more or less than what every clergyman promises to do at his ordination, when he undertakes that his teaching shall be "out of the said Scriptures." He will not use texts from the Bible as pegs on which to hang his ideas, nor will he fall for fanciful interpretations. Again, he will see to it that his sermons, although they may well include illustrations will be something much more than just a string of anecdotes, as some evangelical preaching in past years has been. When we are preaching "out of the Scriptures," we make sure that our hearers can see that the main points that we are making are clearly stated in Scripture, and that what they are hearing is not simply the opinion of the preacher, but the teaching of the Bible.

Many in these days are discovering the value of systematic exposition in which we work through a piece of Scripture Sunday by Sunday. Provided such a series is not too long, it can build up a great deal of interest. Also, it has the advantage that a congregation is delivered from the whims of the preacher, and he may well encounter topics in the course of his exposition which he might never otherwise have chosen for treatment in the pulpit. Some of us find that this is a great economy in the time spent in preparation! Many of us spend a great deal of time in deciding what to preach. If, however, we are already committed to a passage of Scripture, we save this time and can devote it all to the preparation of the actual message. Then another advantage is that with the whole Bible to expound a preacher never dries up! I don't think that without this method I possibly could have survived twelve years in my first benefice.

Now, for one or two suggestions regarding method because, let's face it, some of us find expository preaching far from easy. Perhaps the high ideals with which we began our ministry will have to be sacrificed when we discover that our congregations simply find us boring.

1. Don't attempt too much. Most of us in our days as curates made the mistake of trying to tell people everything we know in one sermon, and undoubtedly some sermons are boring because the preacher tries to say too much. Of course the length of the passage we select will be largely determined by its nature. If it is narrative, we shall probably take a whole story for one sermon; when we are expounding the Epistles, one verse or even half a verse may well be adequate. I often find that I cannot be sure how much ground I am going to cover until I have gotten well ahead with my preparation. Many times when I have been preparing a sermon on a verse, I have discovered I

have accumulated enough material for two sermons. As a result, when my preparation is completed, not only have I finished next Sunday morning's sermon, but I have almost completed one for the Sunday after. Here again we can see clearly the advantage of systematic exposition from Sunday to Sunday.

2. Be certain that the sermon makes one main point on which all else centers. Look, for example, at II Peter 3. Here it may well be possible to take a number of verses for one sermon, because they all center on one point. The question is asked in verse 4, "Where is the promise of his coming?" Here is a sermon on why the second coming of Christ is delayed, and the subsequent verses give us four clear answers to that question.

3. Analyze the sermon into clear points. The example that we have just chosen will exemplify this principle as well. Here is a sermon that has four well-defined sections. The congregation will see the direction in which the preacher is moving, and this is indispensable to holding people's attention and maintaining their interest. It is essential that each point follow logically from the one before.

4. Digest the material yourself. In other words, we should not serve up chunks from old commentaries, although a quotation, if imaginatively introduced, can stimulate interest. Normally, however, the help that we receive from commentaries and other books should be written into our rough notes. We then make our final notes with the books closed and simply our Bible and our rough notes open in front of us.

5. Be relevant. It is important to demonstrate this early in the sermon if we are to arouse interest. Again, let's look at the example we have chosen. It should not be difficult for us to point out that this question (II Peter 3:4) is one that people often raise as they look at the 2,000 years which have elapsed since the first coming of Christ. This is a far more effective way to arouse interest in the sermon than beginning with homiletic fanfares such as, "The other day when I was walking round the parish . . ." We must

also see to it that in our exposition of Scripture we are applying it to people in their situations. Here examples can be of tremendous help, drawn from the pages of Scripture, church history, and biography.

6. Don't just impart information but also warm the heart. Paul says in II Corinthians 5, "The love of Christ constraineth us; because we thus judge..." In other words, not only did he make a judgment on the doctrines of the atonement, but he found that when he had grasped the full significance of the truth it moved his emotions. So let us not be afraid to speak with feeling as we expound God's truth. Then, too, we shall challenge the will. Remember Paul told the young preacher Timothy to "exhort with doctrine," and, when the nature of what we are expounding demands it, this will include an evangelistic thrust.

7. Develop an interesting style. Rhetorical questions followed by a pause to make people think before giving the answer can be very effective. When you introduce a quotation, whether it is from the Bible or some other source, don't just say in the midst of a prosey passage, "As the apostle Paul said..." Rather, speak in a conversational style by saying things like: "Now the apostle Paul has something very significant to say on this matter. Listen to what he says..."

To summarize, then, no one can pretend that the teaching ministry is an easy matter. It requires constant study, and there will be an unending struggle for the time we need. However, it is vital to the well-being of God's people, and the results can be very rewarding.

> O teach me Lord, that I may teach
> The precious things Thou dost impart.

From *TSF Bulletin,* Autumn, 1970. Reprinted by permission.

*Robert L. Saucy*

# 6

# Doing Theology
# for the Church

Not long ago we were informed of a Sunday school teacher who had instructed his class on the doctrine of man in the image of God. In our opinion his conclusion on the subject was extremely questionable, and so we inquired as to the source of his understanding. What had he used for a guide to help in the study of this area? The response was that he had been using only his Bible and a concordance. Now, obviously, these sources are central to the task of expositing God's truth. But the question still may be raised with such a reply: Why was there no use made of some of the many theological discussions of the subject? With a minimal amount of time, this teacher could have compared his thinking with many who have investigated this subject far more extensively than the average church teacher is permitted. But he didn't, and his case is all too typical.

This example is not to cast aspersions on the many faithful teachers in the evangelical church. It is rather to point to the evident fact that theology (and we are here using this term for the various theological disciplines) is not seriously penetrating the church. To be sure, the church is not totally barren of theological concepts, but these often come from sources other than the traditionally recognized theologians. The result is often something less than the finest of evangelical theological thinking and at other times rampant confusion bordering on false doctrine. In a report of a simple biblical literacy test conducted by a pastor for the adults of his church, 63 percent had to be classified as biblically illiterate. There was complete confusion as to the number of converts baptized by Jesus, with answers ranging from none (which is correct) up to 300,000. Jesus was listed as living in the time of Julius Caesar, King Saul, and King Solomon. For the two great commandments, the seventh commandment prohibiting adultery received several votes.[1] While the test concerned primarily Bible knowledge, it can be safely said that theological questions would have fared no better. The tragedy is that there exists not only a situation of biblical and theological ignorance, but that which is undoubtedly its correlative, a lack of concern on the part of many for theology.

A lengthy apologetic need hardly be made among theologians for the necessity or desirability of theology in the church. However, this necessity has not always captured the imagination of the general church member. Too often the attitude is that described by Norman Perrin of the German feeling, "For Germany theological discussion has been, and up to a point still is, the province of the academically trained theologian rather than that of the general lay member of the church."[2] While not all Christians are to be theologians in the sense of being peculiarly summoned to the task of leading in the theological thought, yet according to the Protestant principle of the perspicuity of Scripture and the individual responsibility before God, every believer is in a real sense responsible to be his own theologian. To abdicate the theological domain to specialists either through lack of interest or awe of the technicalities involved is not only harmful but impossible. The truth is that every believer is already a theologian. Accepting Warfield's definition of theology as "that science which treats of God and of the relations between God and the universe,"[3] every believer who knows God and himself therefore partakes of the nature of a theologian making the knowledge of God a part of our world of thought. Since the human mind is not content with chaotic bits of knowledge, the impulse is present in all believers to integrate the revelation of God into their consciousness.

Although it is certainly not the whole of church life, there is a place for a true intellectual love of God and neighbor as well as the love of "heart and soul and strength." Man is also mind. In the words of H. Richard Niebuhr, "The coldness of an intellectual approach unaccompanied by affection is matched by the febrile extravagance of unreasoning sentiment; the aloofness of uncommitted understanding has its counterpart in the possessiveness of unintelligent loyalty. When the whole man is active the mind is also active; when the whole church is at work it thinks and considers no less than it worships, proclaims, suffers, rejoices, and fights."[4]

The intellectual understanding of the faith renders service to the church in many ways. William Barclay in a brief essay entitled "Why Theology?"[5] lists four necessities for its practice. While specialists may take the lead, they cannot perform these requirements vicariously for the church.

1. "Theology is necessary to satisfy the mind." Most at least are not content simply to know and to appropriate the salvation of God in Christ. It must also be understood.

2. "Theology is necessary for teaching and for apologetic purposes." Phillips Brooks once said, "Doctrine is truth considered with reference to being taught." With the significant contemporary evangelistic thrusts of the church, the need of a clear, precise theology was never more urgent. It is improper to be argumentative over the faith, but it is not erroneous to argue for the faith. Peter urges all of his readers to be "ready to make a defense to everyone who asks you to give an account for the hope that is in you" (I Peter 3:15). The words *argue* and *dispute* frequently appear in the ministry of the early Christians in the Book of Acts. In order to enter the ideological fray the believer requires some theological equipment.

3. "Theology is necessary as a test and touchstone." The

church has beliefs and principles by which the allegiance of its members is judged. These beliefs and principles come from theological thinking.

4. Finally, theology is necessary for ethics. It is possible to separate how a man acts and thinks, but not logically or consistently, and not for long. "For as he thinketh in his heart so is he," the biblical writer reminds us. If the church is to live in the world with a lifestyle that issues in glory to God, it must think and think deeply, not only of personal ethics, but of the implications of the biblical faith for social, economic, and political ethics as well. These necessities touch the heart of the church's life and mission; they are not optional peripheries. To the same extent that theological indifference is sustained, the church is vitiated.

But theology is not only mandatory for the healthy functioning of the church, it is postulated by the very nature of the church. If theologians are members of the body of Christ, they have a spiritual ministry even as every member "for the common good" of the body. For an individual to attempt to ignore the theological thought of the church and to begin and end with his own doctrines is to depreciate the manifestations of the Spirit embodied in the life ministries of many of God's servants today as well as down through the history of the church. The revelation of God inscripturated in the Word must always be the immediate object of study. The Bible is the norm of the church and not theology. But to study only the Bible is not only a fraudulent claim, for no one is completely isolated from outside influence, it is a disregarding of the gifts of teaching in the church.

It is not our purpose to explore all of the reasons for the nonchalant attitude of many toward theological studies. Undoubtedly the intellectual and cultural milieu of our day with its antimetaphysical, experience-centered climate contributes much to the nontheological attitude. The popular reporting of theological fadism in the religion columns of newspapers and magazines is certainly also a factor. It does not require an uncanny imagination to see

how many intelligent church people could become disen-
chanted with the theological elite after reading of the de-
mise of God or even the demand to demythologize the
Scriptures. It is perfectly understandable how they might
come to the conclusion that they have a surer grip on God
and His truth than the theologians and need not waste
their time with their speculative musings.

All these reasons aside, however, it is still necessary to
ask the question, are theologians who seek to be faithful
to the Christian faith doing theology for the church?
Granted that the lack of theological acumen on the part of
many church members is due to some factors beyond the
control of the professional theologian, are there factors of
responsibility which also rest upon him? We would like to
suggest that there are and that we need to keep them in
mind in all of our theological endeavor.

Perhaps the fundamental impetus of our thoughts
comes from reading some time ago Michael Green's *Evangelism in the Early Church*[6] in which he points out that the
early theologians were churchmen, and not only churchmen, but evangelists. This is not to say that they were all
good theologians or that contemporary theologians must
be the bishops or what have you of their denominations. It
is only to point out the vital, intrinsic connection between
theology and the church in the era of the rapid spread of
Christianity. Despite the fact that the theological sciences
have advanced and the vast amount of information requires technical specialization as in other areas of knowledge, theology cannot afford to become a sort of esoteric
endeavor done only for the initiated. It is germane to have
theological societies, but unless they operate consciously as
servants of the church little value is forthcoming. One is
reminded somewhat facetiously of the "fat ghost with the
cultured voice," as C. S. Lewis describes him in his work
*The Great Divorce.* Upon refusing to repent of his snobbish
spirit of open-ended intellectual inquiry and enter the
heavenly solid city, he cuts off the conversation with his
host to return to the grey city by saying, "Bless my soul, I'd

nearly forgotten. Of course I can't come with you. I have to be back next Friday to read a paper. We have a little Theological Society down there."

The responsibility of making theology pertinent to the church rests both upon the theologian and the church. It is not our purpose to discuss the situations in the church which may be hindering stimulation in theological interest. We would only submit that the radical separation of clergy and laity, with its attending circumstance in many churches of the authoritative clerical interpretation in theological matters, does little to encourage private study. Our concern here, however, is with the nature of theology done by the theologian for the church. In this respect we would like to suggest three imperatives which surely come to you by way of reminder, but nevertheless require renewed implementation today.

1. Theology must be understandable to the church. In a broadside attack which cannot be denied as totally off target, Robert Brow writes, "For the church at large we have few specialists who can teach through the mass media. Books of Christian doctrine are produced and apparently bought, but one wonders how many of these are readable, let alone stimulating. Our best brains are siphoned off to seminaries where they are expected to write indigestible monographs for the half dozen other men in the world who can understand what they are talking about. In the past doctors of the church wrote so that literate men could understand, and Augustine, Aquinas, Luther, Calvin, and Wesley are much easier to read than our contemporaries. When C. S. Lewis writes theology in his spare time and millions are fed by his books, our theologians still assume that he is shallow because he lacks footnotes, bibliographies, and thesis style. . . . The greatest battle is the battle of the mind, and it is won by words that are shot like bullets—smooth, sharp, powerful, and dead on target."[7]

It is well to remind ourselves that the gospel was written for all men. Even the erudite mind of the great apostle

Paul expressed theological thoughts in words intended for the church to understand. There are no more profound writings in all the world than those of the apostle John with their disclosures of God, man, and the world. Yet they ordinarily become the starting point of Greek language studies because of their plain words. In his introduction to Calvin's *Institutes of the Christian Religion,* McNeill remarks that Calvin frequently commended the biblical writers for their clarity, simplicity and brevity and sought to emulate them in his own writings.[8] It is not in the use of long, technical words that theology produces its impact, but in words which allow the illuminating Spirit of God to most clearly impress the truth upon the mind.

The space program has reminded us that a particular field has a vocabulary all its own. But while other sciences may afford the luxury of their own special verbal symbols, theology cannot. It makes little difference if we understand what ground control says to the astronauts: most of us have no plans to go to the moon. But if theological thought is significant to the Christian way, all believers must understand, for all are travelling together. It may be scientific to say:

> Scintillate, scintillate, globule vivific,
> Fain would I fathom thy nature specific,
> Loftily poised in the ether capacious,
> Strongly resembling a gem carbonaceous.

But it is more communicative to state,

> Twinkle, twinkle, little star
> How I wonder what you are,
> Up above the world so high,
> Like a diamond in the sky.

To be sure, scholarly theological dialogue has value and will not be understood by all. But whatever value it has is in vain unless somehow it is translated into communication for the common man. May it never be said of evangelical theology as Abraham Kuyper says of the eighteenth century theology, that in its impotence it "sought strength in sesquipedalian words and lofty terms. . ."[9]

2. Secondly, theology must be relevant to the church. Lord Eccles, in his book *Half Way to Faith,* points the finger at theological writers when he says, "The laity, although better informed on almost everything else, has never been so ignorant about the ground-plan of the New Testament; this is partly your fault because you have concentrated your scholarships in fields too narrow to be widely interesting; will you now turn your attention to the gospel as a whole? To its relevance as a whole to the age in which we live?"[10]

The various specialized disciplines of theological science are indispensable to an accurate wholeness of truth. Without the scholarship of experts in philology, philosophy, archeology, history, and other related fields, theological study would be seriously impoverished. But if these specializations are pursued for themselves, and not molded into a unified view of truth, they are lost in the satisfaction of scholarly achievement. As in medicine, so in theology there is an increasing need for the general practitioner who can build the parts into a meaningful life system.

It is not our intention to impugn or subvert the validity of those disciplines which are performed on the base of natural empirical studies common to all investigators. But, as Abraham Kuyper correctly pointed out, these studies do not finally touch the higher function of theology. They do not set before the church and the world a system of truth which depends upon the regenerated illumined mind and exposes the radical difference between Christianity and the philosophies of the world.

The great commission of the Lord commanded the church to make disciples of all peoples. This entails evangelism and instruction in the Christian life. These must be the overriding concerns of theology. It must be remembered that the documents of the New Testament were writings of a missionary church, and it is to the credit of the subapostolic leaders that their thinking was also evangelistically oriented. In the words of Michael Green, "the content of their proclamation was none other than the person of Christ. They made use of all the cultural and intellectual pathways which would facilitate the reception of this message . . . their aim . . . remained both simple and direct, to introduce others to Jesus Christ."[11]

In many areas the church is on the move today, and unless theology can aid in the cause it will simply be ignored. The noted Scotch theologian James Denney once said, "I haven't the faintest interest in theology which does not help us to evangelize." One can hardly fault those who take the same position today.

Too often theological effort is used to argue with unbelieving wisdom rather than point men to Christ. The intellectual climate of the day is significant for any evangelistic theology, but a constant concern with the latest philosophies leaves little energy for a positive offensive and also may appear like war on Mars to most people. Evangelical theologians together with evangelical scholars in all disciplines must become more creative in constructing a system of truth which genuinely confronts the world in meaningful terms where people live. If we believe that the truth conforms to reality, we must begin to find new ways of demonstrating it. These demonstrations may at times conflict with the vanguard of intellectual thought on the historical mood, but if they are worked out from the fundamental biblical principles of the nature of man as an individual and social being, they will be relevant.

We have been led to believe that man has become of age. We are told that we must now deal with secular man who no longer believes in God; he only believes what can be empirically verified, all else is meaningless. Theologians have been busy constructing a theology either conforming to this man or attempting to convert him. But sociologist Peter Berger tells us in his insightful little book *A Rumor of Angels*[12] that this man is not so prevalent after all. A study of American students revealed that 80 percent expressed a "need for religious faith," and in Germany 68 percent said they believed in God, while 86 percent admitted to praying. Would it not be more advisable to accept the teaching of the Word on the religious heart of men and approach them with the thought of Paul at Athens? Although not suggesting an evangelical theology, Berger presents other human propensities such as order and hope, which could possibly become inductive starting points for a contemporary evangelistic theology based on the biblical understanding of human existence.

Turning to the realm of Christian instruction, a theology for the church cannot be content with setting forth and defending faith in the great acts of salvation. It must be fleshed out in terms of the dynamics of life. Epistemological issues are foundational and therefore imperative, but people are more often concerned with the reality of faith in experience. Walking in the power of the Spirit, dealing with personal attitudes and interpersonal relationships, these are issues touching men and women in every strata of life. Bernard Ramm states that the most influential force moving pastors to this type of theology is the experience of the failure of simply preaching and teaching about God's great transactions for man and in man. Ramm notes that "enjoying the benefits of the great divine transactions did not do enough for people in handling the problems of their lives and the quality of interpersonal relationships."[13] Without leaving the objective realities of the truth, theology must increasingly elaborate their functional implementation in life. People want theology to interpret actual living and give guidance about it. Without this they lose interest.

A further imperative of theology in its instructive purpose for the church demands that it transcend the confines of "spirituality" and speak to all of life. Barthian neo-orthodoxy proved to be unstable, at least partially because it isolated the religious element of man from the remainder of his mind. It accepted the Kantian dualism of faith and science and refused to bring all of human thought into captivity to Christ. While acknowledging a cosmic dimension of Christ, evangelical theology may also be charged with fostering an epistemological dualism in the church by default. A theology which purports to provide the rationale for all existence, but does not speak to the affairs in which men spend most of their life can hardly be expected to be motivational.

A factor in the success of the early church according to Green was that "their Christ was no ecclesiastical figure, interested only in men's souls. He was the cosmic Christ, the author, sustainer, and final goal of the universe . . . truth was a unity, and it derived from the ultimate reality made personal in him who was Way, Truth, and Life. It was this conviction which nerved them to proclaim the Absolute in a world which was dominated by the Relative in its morals, religion, and concept of history."[14]

This same theology of universal dimensions is desperately needed both for church life and evangelism. There is an interrelation between the knowledge of God and ourselves. Theology therefore must seek to relate to all areas of human endeavor. The task is immense. No one today would dare to say with Justin, "I have endeavored to learn all doctrines. . . ." It can only be done with the cooperation of evangelical scholarship in all fields. The fact that it has not been done adequately still lies in our opinion with the problems pointed out long ago by Abraham Kuyper. Theologians have concentrated almost exclusively on the conflicts between theology and the secular studies, while the Christian scholars in these fields have for the most part operated dualistically, being secular with the head and sacred with the heart. Real advance, Kuyper notes, will only come when Christians with heart and mind united under the power of regeneration devote all their powers of thought to these natural and historical studies. If theology is to be increasingly meaningful both in the church and out, evangelical theologians must enlist their colleagues in the so-called secular fields and get on with this task.

3. Thirdly, and finally, doing theology for the church requires not only that it be understandable to the ordinary literate person and concerned with the issues of his life, but it must be a confessional theology. By the term confessional we do not refer to theology of a creedal nature but to a theology impregnated with the life commitment of the theologian. The author of a recent book gave the following explanation for its writing. He says, "I have spent my entire life as a teacher and a student of Christian theology and have written many books about the subject; now, as I approach my seventieth year, I feel an urgent desire to communicate to the ordinary man or woman, not the professional scholar, what means most to me—not because I have any confidence that I am always right about everything, but because I am sure that people who, like me, are trying to be disciples of Jesus Christ, can be helped when someone a little older tells them what has come to be central in his own life and experience."

Theology, all will agree, aims at nothing short of the transformation of life. But unless it is done in a manner which conveys a genuine experiential dimension, it fails of its goal. The theology which captures the minds of men has always been that which springs from the heart engaged with the practical needs of a living faith. It has been said of Calvin that "in the midst as at the outset of his work, it was the practical preoccupations of living faith which guided him, and never a desire for pure speculation." Theology by its very nature cannot be done as other studies simply for the sake of truth. It cannot rest with the ideas of God and man, sin and salvation. While it deals in I–It relationships, to use Buber's expressions, it urges the participant on to the I–Thou. Unless theology is done with the testimony of the latter relationship, it is unlikely to engender it in its hearers. The note of personal involvement is constantly struck in the New Testament writings and, to cite Green again, it pervaded the works of the early Christians. "Even the most academic of them were convinced that they found the truth in Christ, and were not embarrassed to add their personal testimony to the message they delivered."[16]

In this connection the statement of Donald Bloesch concerning the relative dearth of devotional writings in the new evangelicalism and the need of such works for an impact on the modern church is pertinent to all.[17] Doing theology for the church requires that it be done in the presence of God. The mind must be committed to the laborious task of making the revelation of God a part of a unified world view of conscious thought, and the heart must be surrendered to the experience of it.

Church renewal involves many facets, not the least of which is a renewed love of God with the mind. The challenge lies before us to exercise our spiritual service as a part of the church for the edification of all.

From the *Journal of the Evangelical Theological Society*, vol. 16, 1973. Reprinted by permission.

# Notes to Chapter 6

1. Thomas R. Pendell, "Biblical Literacy Tests," *Christian Century* (October 21, 1959), p. 1213.
2. Norman Perrin, *The Kingdom of God in the Teaching of Jesus* (Philadelphia: Westminster, 1971), p. 35.
3. B. B. Warfield, *Studies in Theology* (London: Oxford Univ. Press, 1932), p. 56.
4. H. Richard Niebuhr, *The Purpose of the Church and Its Ministry* (New York: Harper and Brothers, 1956), p. 111.
5. William Barclay, "Why Theology," in *Faith and Thought, Journal of the Victorian Institute* 97 (Winter 1968): 46–51.
6. Michael Green, *Evangelism in the Early Church* (Grand Rapids: Eerdmans, 1970).
7. Robert Brow, *The Church: An Organic Picture of Its Life* (Grand Rapids: Eerdmans, 1968), p. 71.
8. John T. McNeill, in *Institutes of the Christian Religion,* by John Calvin (Philadelphia: Westminster, 1960), p. lxx.
9. Abraham Kuyper, *Principles of Sacred Theology* (Grand Rapids: Eerdmans, 1963), p. 671.
10. Michael Green, *Man Alive* (Downers Grove, IL: Inter-Varsity, 1967), p. 3.
11. Green, *Evangelism in the Early Church,* p. 276.
12. Peter Berger, *A Rumor of Angels* (Garden City, NY: Doubleday, 1969), pp. 24–25.
13. Bernard Ramm, "Is It Safe to Shift to 'Interpersonal Theology'?" *Eternity* (December 1972), p. 22.
14. Green, *Evangelism in the Early Church,* p. 277.
15. Kuyper, *Principles of Sacred Theology,* p. 608.
16. Green, *Evangelism in the Early Church,* p. 206.
17. Donald Bloesch, "The New Evangelism," *Religion in Life* 41 (Autumn 1972): 335–36.

*Emil Brunner*

# 7

# The Necessity
# for Dogmatics

The urgent question for a humanity which despairs of all truth: "Is there any truth which one can believe at all? And, if so, does Christian doctrine, as such, claim to be truth of this kind?" lies, as we have already seen, outside the sphere of dogmatics. The Christian church deals with this question by means of an intellectual discipline which is closely related to dogmatics, yet which must always be strictly distinguished from it; this study is called "apologetics," a name which is as traditional as the term "dogmatics." Apologetics is the discussion of questions raised by people outside of, and addressed to, the Christian church; therefore at all times it has proved to be as urgent, and as inevitable, as the Christian study of doctrine proper, or dogmatics.

The question of the justification for, and the necessity of, dogmatics differs from the former question because it arises within the church. And yet it is a genuine and not a rhetorical question; nor is it even merely academic. The fact is, this question is justified from the standpoint of the "scientific" theologian. Serious objections have been raised to the whole undertaking, objections which must be recognized; to ignore them would simply mean that we had already fallen a prey to that dogmatic "rigidity," and that overemphasis on the intellectual aspect of doctrine which is so deplorable.

The first objection concerns the loss of directness, and

even of simplicity of faith, which is necessarily connected with the process of dogmatic reflection. A person who has hitherto only encountered the biblical gospel in its simplest form, and has been gripped by it in a direct, personal way, must necessarily feel appalled, chilled, or repelled by the sight of massive volumes of dogmatics, and his first acquaintance with the whole apparatus of ideas and reflection connected with this study of theology as a science. Instinctively the simple Christian murmurs: "But why this immense apparatus of learning? What is the use of these subtle distinctions and these arid intellectual definitions? What is the use of this process of 'vivisection' of our living faith?" When, further, this "simple believer" becomes aware of the theological controversies and passionate dogmatic conflicts which seem inevitable, it is easy to understand that the simple Christian man or woman turns away from all this with horror, exclaiming: "I thank Thee, O Father, Lord of heaven and earth, that Thou didst hide these things from the wise and understanding, and didst reveal them unto babes!" (Matt. 11:25). He sees the contradiction between the simple gospel of the New Testament and this world of extremely abstract conceptions, between the living concreteness of the speech of Jesus and His apostles, which speaks straight to the hearts of all who listen aright, and this ruthless analysis, this massive labor of systematic theology, in which only people of high intellectual gifts can share, which seems to be possible only at the cost of losing the freshness and directness of a living experience. Like a certain French theologian, he says, rightly: "A Gospel which cannot be put on a postcard cannot be the Gospel which was preached to the fishermen of the Lake of Galilee!" From this point of view dogmatics seems to be a perversion of the gospel.

The second objection is closely connected with the first. It is raised by people who feel that the biblical gospel calls them to *action*. Their faith has awakened them to see and feel the sufferings of humanity, the terrible need and the burning questions of their own day, and they feel that "love constrains them" to give the world all the help they possibly can, both inwardly and outwardly. This being so, they feel: "Who would waste time trying to answer such difficult intellectual problems? Dogmatics is theory, but faith is obedience and fellowship. How can we waste time in speculations about the mysteries of the Trinity while there are human beings in trouble—both body and soul!"

This direct and nonreflective rejection of dogmatics by the practical Christian layman is austerely expressed[1] by the philosopher in intellectual terms. Dogmatics, he says, like all theory, belongs to the "sphere of recollection," of reflection, of thought which is concerned with ideas; faith arises in the "reality" of encounter. Between these two there is an impassable gulf. The truth which is given to faith is only understood by one who meets the "Other" in action and in suffering, but it is not understood by the man who seeks truth in the sphere of solitary thought. Therefore the introduction of the truth of faith into that intellectual process of reflection, which is so remote from reality, can do faith no good; indeed, it can only do harm, because it diverts the Christian believer from his real duty of active love to God and his neighbor.

There is another equally important objection. It runs rather like this: "Dogmatics comes from 'dogma.' However, you may define it, still by your precious 'dogma' you want to force us to accept an objective authority, an impersonal doctrinal authority, inserted between us and the Source of faith, Jesus Christ Himself; you want to set up a system of doctrinal coercion, which is in opposition to the freedom of faith. You want to establish an ecclesiastical heteronomy which restricts the liberty of the children of God! You want to repeat the ancient error, and to perpetuate it, that doctrine is the object of faith—a doctrine preserved by the church, on which she bases her clerical authority. Inevitably, dogmatics leads to ecclesiastical

---

1. Cf. E. Grisebach: *Gegenwart; Freiheit und Zucht; Die Schicksalfrage des Abendlandes.*

tyranny, which, more than anything else, obstructs our view of the gospel of the New Testament."

Finally, there is a fourth objection, which represents the views of those who admit the necessity for thinking about the gospel, but who regard dogmatics as a perverted form of such thinking. Those who take this position claim that what the church of our day needs is not a continuance of the dogmatic labors of previous centuries, which, as we know by experience, divides the church by its definitions, but an intellectual effort which, recognizing the peculiar need of our own times, and the widespread lack of faith at the present day, tries to seek to win the outsider by answering his questions, and by entering into a real discussion with him. A dogmatic analysis of ideas does not make the gospel more intelligible to the unbeliever, but less; it does not help him to understand why he ought to accept the Christian faith. The true task of the Christian thinker, however, should be the very opposite—a task which hitherto has only been undertaken by great men who are exceptions in the realm of theology, men like Hamann, Pascal, or Kierkegaard. So long as the church still uses her intellectual powers on the old traditional lines, she is neglecting the one and only important and fruitful intellectual task, which is her real duty.

Faced by these objections, are we to regard the enterprise of dogmatics, in spite of the weighty tradition behind it, as unnecessary? Or even if not actually dangerous, as at least a bypath for the teaching church?

In the following pages the effort will be made to allow the history of the church itself to give the answer to this question. We must, however, begin at this point; namely, that the Bible itself knows nothing of that process which from time immemorial the church has known as "dogmatics." For more than a thousand years Israel existed as a religious community without anything like a system of dogma, in the sense, for instance, in which Calvin uses it in his *Institutes*—indeed, the Jewish church did not even possess a catechism, and even the early Christian church—that is, the Christian church at the time of its highest vitality and purity, did not produce anything of the kind. This fact does make us think. *One* thing it does prove, beyond a doubt, namely, that dogmatics does not belong to the *"esse,"* but at the most to the *"bene esse"* of the church. For the *"esse"* of the church consists only in that without which she could not possibly exist. But the church existed for two hundred years without dogmatics. Thus if dogmatics is under no circumstances an *absolute* necessity, is it perhaps a *relative* necessity? That is, something which, under certain circumstances, is necessary. The history of the church gives a clear affirmative answer to this question—a threefold answer. Dogmatics springs from a threefold source: there are three urgent necessities for dogmatics which spring from the life of the church itself, and cannot be ignored.

(a) The first root of dogmatics is the *struggle against false doctrine*. The sinful self-will of man takes the gospel—at first imperceptibly, and indeed perhaps unconsciously—and alters the content and the meaning of the message of Jesus Christ and His mighty act of redemption, of the kingdom of God and the destiny of man. This produces "substitute" gospels, introduces "foreign bodies" into Christian truth and distorts the Christian message: the very words of the Bible are twisted, and given an alien meaning, and indeed, one which is directly opposed to its purpose. The Christian church is in danger of exchanging its divine treasury of truth for mere human inventions. This being so, ought not those who know the original truth feel called to make a clear distinction between truth and illusion—between "gold" and "cat-gold" (yellow mica)? This necessity of distinguishing between truth and error, and of warning the members of the church against false teaching, makes it quite impossible to adopt the naïve attitude which can ignore these things. Comparison and reflection become necessary and the more subtle and refined are the errors, the more urgent does this become. Where the very words of the Bible have been twisted to mean something different, it is not sufficient to appeal to the "words" of Scripture; where whole systems of alien thought have been "smuggled" into the message of the church, it becomes necessary to set the whole on the one side over against the whole on the other, and to show clearly how each is built up into a system. It is the perversion of doctrine which leads to the formation of the ideas and systems of dogma. It was out of the fight against heresy that the dogmatics of the early church arose; the dogmatics of the Reformation period arose out of the struggles to purify the message of the Bible from Roman Catholic errors.

(b) The second source from which dogmatics is derived is that of catechetical instruction, or preparation for baptism. Even the simplest Christian faith contains a doctrinal element. We have already pointed out that the church never can, and never will be, without doctrine. Even the simple, nontheological teaching of Jesus is full of "theological" content. A person cannot become a Christian without *knowing* something about the Father in heaven, the forgiveness of sins, atonement through the Son of God, and the work of the Holy Spirit; and when he "knows" these biblical phrases he must go further and grasp their inner meaning. The teaching church has to become the church which instructs catechumens. But the thoughtful person cannot receive these doctrines without finding that they raise questions in his mind. The more alert and vigorous is his thinking, the more urgent and penetrating do his questions become. The Christian message must mold and penetrate not only the heart of man, but also his mind, and his processes of thought. But this can only take place if the Christian message is thought out afresh and reformulated in intellectual terms. The thoughtful believer is constantly perceiving new depths and heights in the truth of the gospel. Thus the Christian catechetical instruction which was given through the rich intellectual medium of the Greek world of culture became a method of theological and dogmatic teaching. The instruction of educated catechumens developed into dogmatics.

(c) The third root of dogmatics is that of biblical exegesis. Where there is a living church, a living spiritual life, there men feel the need to penetrate more deeply into the meaning of the Bible, to draw water from the richness of its wells of truth, to enquire into the hidden connections between its main ideas. Such people are not satisfied with an approximate and provisional knowledge—they want something exact and permanent. But this means that when the great "words" of the Bible, such as "sin" or "grace," are studied, it is not enough to study them in the particular passage in question: they must be investigated from the standpoint of biblical doctrine as a whole, and *this,* they feel, they must grasp as a whole. It is not sufficient, for instance, to know what the apostle Paul means by the "righteousness of God" in a particular passage in the Epistle to the Romans: we want to know what he means by this expression as a whole, and also how this specifically Pauline phrase is related to other phrases which, although they sound different, contain a similar meaning in other biblical writers. Then when the biblical scholar has done his work—when he has explained the Epistle to the Romans, and has related it to "Pauline theology" as a whole—then the reader of the Bible, who wants to learn not only from Paul but from the whole revelation contained in Scripture, starts a fresh process of questioning, and it is such questions that the systematic theologian tries to answer. It is at this point that the "Dictionary of the Bible," or the *"loci theologici,"* comes into being.

This threefold root is still visible in the titles of the three standard dogmatic works of the Reformation period. The struggle against heresy is represented by Zwingli's *Commentarious de vera et falsa religione;* the instruction of catechumens by the *Institutio christianae religionis* of Calvin—which developed out of an expanded catechism; the need for a "Dictionary of the Bible" for the Bible reader, by the first dogmatic work of Melanchthon, his *Loci theologici.*

For the sake of the gospel the church cannot ignore its duty to distinguish false doctrine from true; to this end it must make the effort to express the content of its simple teaching in more exact and thoughtful terms. The church must help the reader of the Bible by giving him a comprehensive explanation of the chief biblical terms; church leaders cannot ignore the fact that it is their duty to give thoughtful members of the Christian community a body of instruction which goes further than the most elementary elements of the faith, and to answer their questions. Hence the church cannot fail to develop her doctrine in the sense of giving more exact and precise definitions of ideas; then, she must show the connection of these ideas with the whole body of Christian truth. This process is "dogmatics." This is the answer from church history.

But this historical answer alone is not sufficient; primarily, because it starts uncritically from an historical position which is not impregnable; that is, it assumes that the original doctrine of the church was clear and uniform.

The New Testament is not a book of doctrine, but it is a collection of apostolic confessions of faith and historical records which have been written down in order to awaken and strengthen faith. But in these believing testimonies to God's revelation in Jesus Christ there is already a good deal of intellectual and theological reflection—in some more, and in others less. From this it is possible to construct a "theology of the apostles"—as we shall see later on—and this New Testament doctrine will become the basis of all dogmatic instruction. Now however, this process of development—from the relatively nonreflective, immediate character of the doctrine of the New Testament, to the highly developed doctrinal system of the church, proves to be inevitable, because this "theology of the apostles" is not an absolute unity, but is presented in a series of different types of doctrine, which differ considerably from one another. In a variety of doctrine the one Christ and the one gospel bear witness to the divine act of redemption. The fact that this "unity" exists within a partly contradictory multiplicity evokes critical reflection. It is not the task of the church to teach what Matthew, Paul, or John teach, but it *is* her duty to proclaim the Word of God;

therefore she must teach the one divine truth in these differing apostolic doctrines. If there were an absolutely uniform, and therefore unmistakably "apostolic doctrine," or "doctrine of the New Testament," then perhaps the work of dogmatics might be superfluous. But since this is not the case, and since the truth of revelation must be sought in and behind the unity of the different testimonies to Christian truth, the work of reflection upon dogma is indispensable.

Hence a simple reproduction of "the" doctrine of the Bible is impossible. Every theology or proclamation of the church which claims to be able to do this is based upon a fiction; in actual fact it is accomplished by an unconscious, and unacknowledged process of systematization of theology. The teachers or preachers of the church who claim for themselves and others that "*they* have no dealings with theology, but that they stick quite simply to the teaching of the Bible" deceive themselves and others. Whatever the church teaches, she teaches on the basis of a normative decision—even though this decision may have taken place unconsciously—concerning the nature of "sound doctrine." Open and honest consideration of sound doctrine can never end in appealing to any "standard" doctrine. Sound doctrine, when more closely examined, always proves to be a task which is never ended, and it is never something which exists "ready-made." Even behind the most primitive forms of Christian teaching, behind the teaching of Jesus and of the apostles, sound doctrine is always something which has to be sought. If the New Testament witness to revelation is the basis and the content of all dogmatics, then its necessity has already been proved by the fact that the task of discovering the unity of sound doctrine behind the different doctrines of the New Testament is unavoidable. Thus the truth of revelation and human doctrine do not only diverge in the sphere of dogmatic reflection, but this contradiction exists already, even in the simplest biblical witness to revelation and faith. Here already it is evident that the divine truth is a light which cannot be received by the human mind without being refracted. The one truth of Christ is refracted in the manifold doctrines of the apostles; but it is the task of the church—which has to proclaim the truth of Christ, and thus also has to teach—to seek continually for the one Light of truth within these refractions. Dogmatics is the science which enables the church to accomplish this task.

Reprinted with permission of Westminster Press, from *The Christian Doctrine of God* by Emil Brunner. Translated by Olive Wyon. Copyright 1950 by W. L. Jenkins.

*Francis Pieper*

# 8

# Nature and Character of Theology

## Christian Religion and Christian Theology

In ecclesiastical terminology a distinction is made between Christian religion and Christian theology, religion (in the subjective sense) designating the knowledge of God and divine matters which all Christians have, and theology (in the subjective sense), the special knowledge of the teachers of the church. We can accept this distinction. Scripture teaches (a) that all Christians have a knowledge of divine matters, for "they shall be all taught of God" (John 6:45); and (b) that the teachers of the church should possess a special knowledge.[1] But there is no difference between these two kinds of knowledge as to their source. The teachers derive their knowledge of God and divine things from the very same source from which all other Christians derive it—from Holy Scripture. There is no other source open to theologians.

Modern theologians are not agreed on the relation between "religious" and "theological" knowledge. Some want to "connect them as closely as possible," while others want to separate them as widely as possible. At the present time much is being written on the difference between "religious" and "theological" knowledge.[2] According to the scriptural, the Christian, standard we must maintain that "religious knowledge" and "theological knowledge" do not differ essentially regarding source and medium of cognition. That is to say, theological knowledge begins and ends where all the knowledge of all Christians begins and ends—by believing the Word of God as we have it in Scripture. The theologians, the teachers of the church, do not progress in their knowledge of the Christian doctrine one inch beyond God's revelation in His Word. That is the clear teaching of Scripture.[3]

The textbooks in which the divine knowledge of all Christians is systematically arranged according to the chief parts of the Christian religion (religion in the objective sense, as doctrine) are usually called catechisms, *Religionslehre,* handbooks of the Christian doctrine, etc.[4] The manuals in which the special divine knowledge of the teachers of the church (theology in the objective sense) is presented are called: Textbooks of Theology, Dogmatics, Systematic Theology, Scientific Theology, *die christliche Lehre in wissenschaftlicher Darstellung,* etc. . . . formerly *loci communes, systema theologiae Christianae,* etc. May the terms "science" and "system" be applied to theology? Yes and no. Because of its importance this matter will be discussed at length in the chapters "Theology and Science" and "Theology and System."

## Christian Theology

The etymology of "theology" is not doubtful, as is the case with the term "religion." The original meaning of *theologia* is clearly *logos peri tou theou.* Theology denotes, in its subjective sense, the knowledge of God and of divine matters: in its objective sense it designates the doctrine of God.[5] Analogous terms are psychology, physiology, biology, astrology, etc. Thomas Aquinas: *"Theologia a Deo docetur, Deum docet, et ad Deum ducit."* Similarly Baier: "In the composite term *theology* the name *theou* denotes the object of the *logos"* (Baier-Walther, I, 2).

As to the usage (*usus loquendi*) of the term "theology," we note that it does not occur in Holy Writ. Our old theologians say: "Theology is a word not *engraphos,* but *agraphos;*

however, it is not *antigraphos.*" In the heading of the Book of Revelation, St. John is indeed called "the theologian" (*"apokalupsis Iōavvou tou theologou"*), but, as Gerhard points out, "whoever wrote this heading gave John this title, not he himself." Note further that the terms "theology" and "theologian" did not originate with the Christians. Even the heathen employed these terms. The fact need not surprise us. Knowing that there is a God (Romans 1 and 2), the heathen would naturally devote earnest study to this subject. In their way they studied "theology." And they employed this very term.[6] Calov: "We see that the term *theology* was first used by the heathen and then adopted by the Church" (*Isagoge,* 2d ed., I, 8).

Within the Christian church the word *theology* and its cognate *theologian* are not always used in the same sense. The reminder is here in place that since these terms are not found in Scripture but belong to the vocabulary of the church, there should be no strife about words. What matters is that the words used should not express any unscriptural ideas. The matter denoted by these words must be contained in Scripture. And that is the case when the church takes *theology* to mean:

1. The special measure of the knowledge of God and the divine doctrine which public ministers in the congregation should possess. Scripture speaks of this form of theology when it says that the *episkopos,* who takes care of the church of God (I Tim. 3:5), must be *didaktikos,* "apt to teach" (I Tim. 3:2). The pastor must have a special teaching ability. This matter will be discussed at length in the next chapter.[7]

2. The knowledge of God and the divine doctrine which is required of those who train the future public teachers. These "theological professors" are called theologians in a special sense. Timothy performed the work of a theological professor when he committed the things he had learned from the apostle Paul "to faithful men, who shall be able to teach others also" (II Tim. 2:2).[8]

3. The knowledge of God and the divine doctrine pos-

sessed by all Christians. Luther on this point: "These are words ('For God so loved the world,' etc., John 3:16) which no one can exhaust or fathom; and when they are rightly believed, they ought to make one a good theologian, or rather a strong, happy Christian, who can speak and teach aught of Christ, judge all other doctrines, counsel and comfort all men, and patiently bear all ills" (St. L. XI: 1103).[9]

4. The knowledge and doctrine of certain parts of the Christian religion, namely, of the deity of Christ and, respectively, of the Trinity.[10] This use of the term *theology* has been and is quite general. We, too, call the doctrine of the deity of Christ and of the Trinity "theology in the narrower sense" to distinguish it from cosmology, anthropology, Christology, ecclesiology, etc.

We may use the terms *theology* and *theologia* in this fourfold sense, since the matter itself is found in Scripture. But it is an unscriptural use of language when men define theology as a knowledge of God and divine things which, it is claimed, reaches farther than faith in the Word of Scripture and expands faith into scientific comprehension. This is the *prōton pseudos* of modern theology in all of its various forms. And we have to keep on insisting that when men imagine that their theological knowledge rises above faith in the written Word, they are deluding themselves; their alleged knowledge is ignorance.

Following the custom of the early Lutheran theologians, we shall here use the term *theology* to denote the divine knowledge necessary for the administration of the public ministry. Theology, then, taken subjectively, or concretely, is the aptitude *(hikanotēs habitus)* wrought by the Holy Ghost in a Christian to perform the functions of the pastoral office, i.e., to teach the Word of God, the Word of Scripture, in all its purity, both publicly and privately, to refute all false doctrine and thus to lead sinners to faith in Christ and to salvation.[11] Theology taken objectively as doctrine is the Christian doctrine in its correct oral and written presentation by the public minister of the church.[12] Both definitions are contained, in substance, in Scripture. The subjective concept of theology is found in II Corinthians 3:5–6: "Our sufficiency [*hikanotēs:* ability] is of God, who also hath made us able ministers of the new testament." We have the objective concept, for example, in II Timothy 1:13: "Hold fast the form of sound words which thou hast heard of me."[13] More on these definitions in the following chapters.

Obviously the first and proper meaning of the term *theology* is theology in the subjective sense, aptitude (*hikanotēs*); only in its secondary, derived meaning does it denote objective theology, doctrine. For, as Walther says: "Theology must first be in the soul of a man before he can teach it, present it in speech and writing" (*Lehre und Wehre*, 14, p. 9).[14]

## Theology As Aptitude

Theology in the sense of aptitude, or "personal qualification," is defined in all those Scripture passages which describe the persons to whom according to God's will and ordinance the teaching office in the church may be committed. Walther, following the earlier Lutheran theologians, correctly says: "Since theology, in the subjective sense, is the proficiency which the incumbents of the teaching office in the church should possess, it is clear that when Scripture describes the true teacher, it describes the true theologian" (*Lehre und Wehre*, 14, p. 10). These qualifications are described in Scripture as follows:

1. The theological aptitude is a spiritual aptitude (*habitus spiritualis, supernaturalis*), that is to say, an aptitude which in every case presupposes, besides natural gifts, personal faith in Christ (faith in the forgiveness of sins by grace for the sake of Christ's *satisfactio vicaria*). In other words, it presupposes the conversion of the theologian. Unbelievers may be able to apprehend the whole body of Christian doctrine intellectually, and they may be endowed

with a natural ability to teach it. But that does not make them theologians in the scriptural sense. There is no *"theologia irregenitorum."*[15] Scripture distinctly states that the aptitude to administer the public teaching office is not a natural gift and attainment, but that it is of a spiritual nature, a gift of God: "Not that we are sufficient of ourselves to think any thing as of ourselves, but our sufficiency is of God, who also hath made us able ministers of the new testament" (II Cor. 3:5–6). And all unbelievers are dwelling places and workshops, not of the Holy Ghost, but of the prince of this world: "In times past ye walked according to the prince of the power of the air, the spirit that now worketh in the children of disobedience" (Eph. 2:2). Note, too, that when Scripture speaks of the qualifications for the public ministry, it always describes the minister as possessing not only the special pastoral gifts, but also the common Christian virtues; it invariably describes him as a Christian. For example, according to I Tim. 3:1 ff. the *episkopos* must not only be "apt to teach" (*didaktikos*), but also must "not be given to wine," etc. And in II Tim. 2:1 ff. the aptitude to administer the public ministry is traced back to the grace of God in Christ. "Thou, therefore, my son, be strong in the grace of God that is in Christ." Unbelievers hold the office of the public ministry only by God's toleration, against God's will and ordinance. A remark: it can and will happen that men are converted and saved through the ministry of an unconverted preacher, provided that he preaches the truth of God's Word. The reason for this is that the efficacy of the means of grace is not affected by the character of the administrant.

Our old theologians expressed the truth that the theological aptitude always presupposes personal Christianity by defining this aptitude as *habitus spiritualis, supernaturalis, theosdotos, a Spiritu Sancto per verbum Dei collatus.* Baier, for instance, says: "Theology, then, is essentially a supernatural aptitude, acquired by the powers of grace and through the operation of the Holy Spirit, the theologian himself, of course, making use of these powers"

(Baier-Walther I, 69) and then adds the remark that a "theology" which consists merely in an external knowledge and teaching of the Scripture truth and lacks the "genuine," "supernatural" assent wrought by the Holy Ghost, a theology which unregenerate, wicked man may have, is called theology only in an improper sense.[16] Luther on the *spiritual* character of the theological aptitude: "We see that there is more of heathen and human conceit than of the holy, sure teaching of Scripture in the writings of the theologians. What shall we do about it? The only advice I can give is to humbly pray God that He would give us doctors of theology. The Pope, emperor, and the universities can make doctors of art, of medicine, of jurisprudence, of the Sentences; but be assured that no one can make a doctor of Holy Scripture for you but only the Holy Ghost from heaven, as Christ says in John 6:45: "They shall be all taught of God" (St. L. X:339 f). An important element of the spiritual aptitude is, of course, the Christian conviction that the Holy Scriptures are the infallible Word of God, a conviction wrought by the Holy Ghost through the Word of Scripture. Let us elaborate this point at once.

2. The theological aptitude includes the ability of the theologian to confine himself in his teaching entirely to God's Word; he must be able to suppress his own thoughts about God and divine matters and put aside the thoughts of other men, deriving the doctrine exclusively from the Word of God, from Holy Scripture. The theologian who refuses to do this is, in the words of St. Paul, a bloated ignoramus *(tetuphōtai, mēden epistauevos)*. "If any man teach otherwise and consent not to the wholesome words, even the words of our Lord Jesus Christ . . . he is proud, knowing nothing" (I Tim. 6:3). And bear in mind that the "words of our Lord Jesus Christ," according to John 17:20, I Peter 1:10–12, Ephesians 2:20, are the writings of the apostles and prophets. Scripture thus declares all those to be theologically incompetent and disqualified for the Christian ministry who are not willing to take their doctrine exclusively from Holy Scripture, but in addition set up

other sources, such as alleged private revelations ("en-thusiasm"), the so-called "Christian consciousness," "faith consciousness," "the regenerate Ego," "the Christian ex-perience," the decretals of the Pope and of "the Church," "history," and so forth. Let us hear Luther on this point: "Jeremiah has an entire chapter on the false prophets (Jeremiah 23). Among other things he says this (v. 16): 'Thus saith the Lord of Hosts, Hearken not unto the words of the prophets that prophesy unto you: they make you vain [they teach you vanity, R.S.V.]: they speak a vision of their own heart—and not out of the mouth of the Lord!' Behold, all prophets who do not preach out of the mouth of the Lord are deceivers, and God forbids us to hear them. Does not the text state clearly that where God's Word is not preached no one dare, under pain of God's wrath, listen to it, for it is pure deception? O Pope, O bishops, O priests, O monks, O theologians, how are you going to escape here? Do you consider it a trifling matter when the Supreme Majesty forbids whatever does not pro-ceed out of the mouth of the Lord and is something else than *God's Word?* It is not a thresher or herdsman who is saying this. When the servant hears the master say: 'Who told you to do that? It is not what I have commanded,' he will certainly realize that he should not have done it as being contrary to the master's orders" (St. L. XIX:821 f.).

3. Another theological skill is the ability to teach the whole Word of God, the entire truth of Scripture. Only he is an able minister of the church who can say with the apostle Paul: "I have not shunned to declare unto you all the counsel of God" (Acts 20:27). If the minister fails to do this, souls entrusted to his care may be eternally lost. Only he who declares all the counsel of God can say with the apostle: "I am pure from the blood of all men" (Acts 20:26). Let us remind ourselves in this connection that since God requires the theologian to teach the entire Christian doctrine without subtraction or addition, "pub-licly and from house to house," therefore theological stu-dents should apply themselves very diligently to acquire

the theological fitness, and pastors in office should strive to retain and increase it. The apostle admonishes Timothy and all theologians: "Take heed unto thyself and unto the doctrine; continue in them; for in doing this thou shalt both save thyself and them that hear thee" (I Tim. 4:16).

4. Again, only he is a fit minister of the church who is able to refute false teachers. This is listed as one of the necessary qualifications of an elder or bishop: "Holding fast the faithful word as he hath been taught, that he may be able by sound doctrine both to exhort and to convince the gainsayers.... whose mouths must be stopped" (Titus 1:9-11). The popular demand that the public teacher refrain from polemics is not supported by Scripture. Scripture admonishes pastors to "avoid foolish questions, and genealogies, and contentions, and strivings about the law; for they are unprofitable and vain" (Titus 3:9).[17] Nor dare we engage in polemics from carnal motives, in carnal zeal. "For though we walk in the flesh, we do not war after the flesh" (II Cor. 10:3). It is also to be noted that in Titus 1:9 the words "able by sound doctrine to exhort" precede "able to convince the gainsayer." That means that the clear presentation of the true doctrine must come before the refutation of the false doctrine. The hearers will thus be in a position to see that the polemics are *justified* and will be able to make the condemnation of the false doctrine their own. And they will hardly suspect the teachers of being contentious and unjust. Scripture thus warns us against false doctrine and rebuking false teachers is laid upon the teachers of the church in Titus 1:9-11 and many other passages of Scripture. All prophets and apostles and Christ Himself have both proclaimed the true doctrine and condemned the false doctrine.

Walther does not go too far when he writes: "A man may proclaim the pure doctrine, but if he does not condemn and refute the opposing false doctrine, does not warn against the wolves in sheep's clothing, the false prophets, and unmask them, he is not a faithful steward of God's mysteries, not a faithful shepherd of the sheep entrusted to him, not a faithful watchman on the walls of Zion, but, as the Word of God says, an unfaithful servant, a dumb dog, a traitor. The terrible consequences of the minister's failure to use the *elenchus* are before our eyes—many souls lost and the church deeply hurt. Polemics are absolutely needed. Not only because a doctrine is more fully comprehended in the light of its antithesis, but mainly because the errorists so craftily mask their error behind a show of truth that the simple Christians, if not forewarned, are despite their love of the truth only too easily deceived. The pastor cannot wash his hands in innocence, pleading that he has always preached the full truth, if he did not at the same time warn against the error and, when necessary, identify it by naming the errorist; if his sheep, either while he is still serving or after he had to leave them for another field, become the prey of the ravening wolves in sheep's clothing, he is guilty of their blood" (Walther, *Pastorale,* p. 82 f. [Fritz, *Pastoral Theology,* 1945, p. 336 f.]).

When men here invoke the "spirit of tolerance," we must remind them of the difference between church and state. Tolerating false teachers in the state is something different from tolerating them in the church. The Christian church of the New Testament has no command to expel false teachers from the state or the civil community that would call for the use of force, and the church is enjoined from employing force. But the church may not tolerate the false teachers in the church. God has commanded the church to take up arms against them and oppose them with the Word of God. This means that the church must (a) realize that he who departs from the Word of the apostles is a false teacher (Rom. 16:17: "Mark them which cause divisions and offences contrary to the doctrine which ye have learned"); must (b) disprove their teaching (Titus 1:9, 11: "Convince [convict] the gainsayers. . . . whose mouths must be stopped"); and finally (c) must isolate them, that is, having no church fellowship with them (Rom. 16:17: "Avoid them"; II John 10; "neither bid him God speed"), and eventually, if they do not themselves sever their connection with the church, formally excommunicate them (I Tim. 1:20: Hymenaeus and Alexander expelled from the church; cf. II Tim. 2:17; 4:14).

5. The theological aptitude includes, finally, the willingness and strength to suffer for the Christian doctrine. Scripture distinctly includes the readiness to suffer for the sake of Christ and His Word as a necessary part of the theologian's equipment. The apostle Paul tells Timothy: "Thou therefore endure hardness ["hardship," R.S.V.] as a good soldier of Jesus Christ," "suffer trouble even unto bonds" (II Tim. 2:3, 9). The minister of the gospel cannot escape trouble because the gospel, which he preaches, salvation by faith in the crucified Christ without the deeds of the law, does not at all appeal to the world, but is "a stumblingblock to the Jews and foolishness to the Greeks" (I Cor. 1:23). The Christians' lot, therefore, is described by Christ Himself: "Ye shall be hated of all nations for my name's sake" (Matt. 24:9). It is but natural—and experience confirms it—that this hatred should be directed principally against the teachers of the church. What Jesus said concerning Paul applies in some degree to all faithful ministers of the gospel: "I will show him how great things he must suffer for my name's sake" (Acts 9:16; cf. Acts 26:21). And if the minister is not willing to suffer the loss of his goods, of honor and rank, yes, even of his life, he is not a profitable servant of the church: he will, for the sake of ease, compromise with error; he may even deny Christ, and thus be denied by Him (II Tim. 2:12). The Christian ministry requires strong men, men able to "endure hardship": "Thou therefore, my son, be strong in the grace that is in Christ Jesus" (II Tim. 2:1).

Reprinted with permission of Concordia Publishing House, from *Christian Dogmatics*, vol. 1, by Francis Pieper. Copyright 1950 by Concordia Publishing House.

# Notes to Chapter 8

1. The rhetorical question: "Are they all teachers?" (I Cor. 12:29) means that not all Christians are teachers. According to I Tim. 3:2 one who would be a bishop must be *didaktikos,* "apt to teach," have a special degree of the ability to teach, for, according to verse 5, he is to take care not only of himself and his own house, but also of the church of God. Paul stresses this once more in II Tim. 2:2: "The things that thou hast heard of me among many witnesses, the same commit thou to faithful men, who shall be able to teach others also." Therefore men must not be elected to the teaching office by lot or in any other haphazard way; only such may be chosen as possess the qualifications set down in I Tim. 3:1 ff.; Titus 1:5-11, one of which is a special aptitude to teach.

2. See, for instance, Richard Gruetzmacher, *Studien zur dogm. Theol.,* 3, p. 120 ff.

3. According to John 8:31-32 the knowledge of the truth is mediated by the Word of Christ, which we have in the Word of His apostles (John 17:20): "If ye continue in my word . . . ye shall know the truth." And only by believing Christ's Word do men "continue in it." When a teacher does not continue in Christ's Word, the apostle does not credit him with knowledge but with ignorance (I Tim. 6:3-4).

4. Cf. Zezschwitz, R. E., 2d ed., VII, 585 ff. Luther in his "Short Preface" to the Large Catechism defines a catechism as an "instruction for children and the simpleminded," as an "instruction for children, what every Christian must needs know, so that he who does not know this could not be numbered with the Christians, nor be admitted to any Sacrament" (*Trigl.* 575). Cf. F. Bente, in *Concordia Triglotta,* "Historical Introductions," pp. 62-93, on catechisms in general and Luther's catechism in particular, also for a bibliography of recent literature.

5. Luthardt, *Kompendium,* p. 4. Walther, *Lehre und Wehre,* 14, 5. Augustine, *De Civ. Dei,* VIII, 1: "We understand the Greek *theologia* to mean the knowledge and doctrine of the deity" *(ratio sive sermo).*

6. Aristotle says that Thales and those who before him speculated on the origin of things "theologized," *theologēsantes* (*Metaph.* I, 3). According to Josephus, Pherekydes of Syros in the sixth century wrote a book with the title *Theologia,* in which he philosophized about the heavens and things divine (*C. Apion,* I, 2). Cicero writes: "In the beginning there were three Joves—so say those who are called theologians" (*De Nat. Deorum* III, 21). Augustine quotes Varro, a contemporary of Cicero, on

three types of heathen theology: "The mythical genus, used mostly by the poets; the physical, used by the philosophers and the civil, which the people and the priests should know and employ" (*De Civ. Dei*, VI, 5). Study Augustine's criticism of the heathen theology in this and the following chapters. See further Buddeus, *Inst.*, 1741, p. 48 sqq.; August Hahn, *Lehrbuch d. Chr. Gl.*, 2d ed., I, 104 f; Walther, *Lehre und Wehre*, 1868, pp. 5 f.

7. Quenstedt I, 13: "*Theologia acroamatica* teaches and establishes the mysteries of the faith and refutes the errors contrary to the sound doctrine more accurately and copiously, and is the province of the bishops and preachers in the Church." According to Koenig, theology is divided into: '*catechetical*, or simple, such as is required of all Christians, and *acromatic*, or more accurate, which is the province of the learned, the ministers of the Word.'"

8. Quenstedt, I, 13: "*Theologia acroamatica* is the province of those who in the seminaries instruct, not Christians but the *future teachers of the Christians;* and these are called theologians *kat' exochēn.*" Luther has some interesting remarks on the theological doctorate. He calls the pomp and ceremony connected with the conferring of this degree "*Larven,*" mummeries. But he does not condemn the thing outright. It is all right if the recipients of the high degree recognize that while the thing in itself means nothing, the honor conferred on them is the honor of the "service in the Word" (St. L. XXI a:564. II:260).

9. Luther also calls the centurion at Capernaum a "*theologus*" because he "argued in such a fine Christian way that one who has been a doctor for four years could not have done better" (St. L. XII:1185). And on Romans 12:7 Luther comments: "Hence you will perceive whom Paul makes doctors of Holy Scripture, namely, all who have the faith, and no one else. They should judge all doctrine, and their decision must stand, even though it be against the Pope, the councils and all the world" (St. L. XII:335). Gerhard, too, says that the term *theology* is used "for the Christian faith and religion as it is found in all believers, the learned as well as the unlearned, and in this sense all who know and accept the articles of faith" (*locus* "De Natura Theologiae," 4), "who teach and profess these articles" (*locus* "De Ministerio Ecclesiastico," 64) are called theologians. According to I Peter 3:15, Colossians 3:16, etc., it is the business of the Christians in general to teach and profess the Christian faith and religion. There are those among the so-called laymen whose knowledge of the Christian doctrine and whose interest in the affairs of the church exceeds the average. We like to call them "lay theologians." The apostolic church had such lay theologians. The list of greetings in Romans 16 seems to indicate that. In the vast majority of cases the lay theologians have proved a blessing to the church. *Lehre und Wehre*, 1860, p. 352, shows that the fear of having "laymen at the synodical conventions" is unwarranted.

10. Thus Gregory Nazianzen (d. ca. 390) was called *ho theologos* because in speech and writing he had so ably defended the doctrine of the deity of Christ. And we know that the church fathers called John *ho theologos* because his Gospel lays particular stress on the eternal, essential

deity of Christ. Thus Athanasius (4th century): "As also the theologian says: 'In the beginning was the Word.'" The church fathers distinguished between theology as the doctrine of the deity of Christ and *oikonomia* (*dispensatio*) as the doctrine concerning the incarnate Christ. Thus Gregory Nazianzen: "The doctrine of the theology or of the nature is one thing, the doctrine of the economy is another." By reason of this specific sense of *theologia* the verb *theologein*, to theologize, came to be used in the sense of "confessing as God." Thus Athanasius: "How can you theologize the Spirit (confess the Spirit as God) if you are not ready to say that He has the same essence and glory, will and power, as the Father and the Son?" (*De S. Trin.*, dial. 3. Opp. ed. Bonutius II, 190 sq. Quoted by Walther in *Lehre und Wehre*, 1868, p. 7.) Basilius uses the word *theology* to designate the doctrine of the mystery of the Trinity: "Had we not better remain silent lest the dignity of theology be endangered because of the poverty and weakness of the language?" (*Sermo de fide et trinitate.* Opp. I, 371. *Lehre und Wehre*, 1868, p. 8.)

11. Quenstedt: "Theology taken concretely as a *habitus* is the God-given practical aptitude of the mind which the Holy Ghost bestows upon a man through the Word, for the purpose of leading sinful man to faith in Christ, and to eternal salvation" (Systema I, 16 ). Similarly Gerhard (*locus* "De Natura Theologiae," 31).

12. Quenstedt: "Theology taken abstractly as a system is the body of doctrine taken from the Word of God, by which men are correctly instructed in faith and life unto salvation; in other words, it is the doctrine drawn from the divine revelation that shows how men are to be trained for the service of God through Christ unto eternal life" (I, 16).

13. "Can you imagine St. Paul writing a normative dogmatics after the manner of Hutter's *Compendium Locorum Theologicorum*?" Thus the advocates of "academic freedom." It is a cheap quip and falls flat in the light of II Timothy 1:13. The passage states very clearly, first, that Timothy heard *hugiainontes logoi* (sound words) from the apostle, words that did not express unsound human opinions, but the pure divine truth; and secondly, that Paul set these "sound words" before Timothy not as matter of passing entertainment or mere amusement, but as the *hupotupōsis*, copy, model, pattern, *norma sanorum verborum*, by which Timothy should be guided in his teaching. Note also the *eche*, "hold," "hold fast"; Timothy is not at liberty to depart from the norm set up by Paul. According to this text, then, Paul did write what we would call a "Normal-dogmatik." Plitt on our passage: "What I have given you use as a pattern, namely, the sound words, 'the sound doctrine' (Titus 1:9)." Matthies: "*hupotupōsis*, pattern, as in I Timothy 1:16, distinct type, original and model." Huther (Meyer's Commentary) remarks: "Luther translates *hupotupōsis*, by 'pattern' (so, too, De Wette, Wiesinger, and others), but this definition is not in the word itself." But the words of the text plainly show that Paul is referring to a "pattern." The *hupotupōsis*, by which men are to be guided becomes *eo ipso* a pattern.

14. Musaeus: "The doctrine regarding God and divine matters issues from the theological aptitude and is its result" (*Introd. in Theol.* 1679, p. 3). Luthardt holds that the old Lutheran theologians, who defined

theology *primo loco* as a personal aptitude, "a personal qualification," meant well, but finds that "this definition is scientifically incorrect" (*Komp.*, 10th ed., p. 4). We fail to see why this definition should be out of line with scientific thinking. Why, Luthardt himself thinks along the same lines! When he with Kahnis defines theology as "the scientific self-consciousness of the church," he, too, conceives of theology as a "personal qualification," since every kind of "self-consciousness," including the "scientific" kind, presupposes persons, in whom it inheres as a *personal* attribute. An impersonal self-consciousness is a contradiction in itself. Luthardt will not deny that he, too, has in mind persons within the church, viz., the theologians who, in distinction from the ordinary Christians, possess a scientific self-consciousness. It is a queer thing by the way, that Luthardt, while thinking of theologians, should define theology as "the scientific self-consciousness of the church." The theologians, whether they are equipped with scientific self-consciousness or not, are not the church.

15. Cf. Walch, *Bibliotheca Theol.*, II, 667, sqq.; Baumgarten, *Theol. Streitigkeiten*, III, 425 f.; there is a wealth of material on the controversy concerning this point in Hollaz., *Examen Prol.*, I, qus. 18–21.

16. It is not correct to say that Spener was the first to emphasize this truth. In his tract "Die Allgemeine Gottesgelehrtheit" Spener himself says that others have done that before him. (See Baier, *loc. cit.*)

17. Quenstedt: "In the field of polemical theology we must take special care not to engage in controversies over useless questions and not to let controversies breed controversies; polemics must not become a quarrelsome and contentious theology, by which the truth is lost through too much disputing" (*Systema* I, 14).

# 9

# The Importance of Christian Knowledge

*For when for the time ye ought to be teachers, ye have need that one teach you again, which be the first principles of the oracles of God; and are become such as have need of milk, and not of strong meat.*
*Hebrews 5:12*

These words are a complaint, which the apostle makes against the Christian Hebrews, for their want of such proficiency in the knowledge of the doctrines and mysteries of religion, as might have been expected of them. The apostle complains, that they had not made that progress in their acquaintance with the things taught in the oracles of God, which they ought to have made. And he means to reprove them, not merely for their deficiency in spiritual and experimental knowledge of divine things, but for their deficiency in a doctrinal acquaintance with the principles of religion, and the truths of Christian divinity; as is evident by the manner in which the apostle introduces this reproof. The occasion of his introducing it is this: In the next verse but one preceding, he mentions Christ as being "called of God an high priest after the order of Melchizedek." In the Old Testament, the oracles of God, Melchizedek was held forth as an eminent type of Christ; and the account we there have of him contains many gospel mysteries. These mysteries the apostle was willing to point out to the Christian Hebrews; but he apprehended, that through their weakness in knowledge, they would not understand him; and therefore breaks off for the present from saying any thing about Melchizedek, thus (v. 11.), "Of whom we have many things to say, and hard to be uttered; seeing ye are all dull of hearing"; i.e. there are many things concerning Melchizedek which contain wonderful gospel mysteries, and which I would take notice of to you, were it not that I am afraid, that through your dullness, and backwardness in understanding these things, you would only be puzzled and confounded by my discourse, and so receive no benefit; and that it would be too hard for you, as meat that is too strong.

Then come in the words of the text: "For when for the time ye ought to be teachers, ye have need that one teach you again which be the first principles of the oracles of God; and are become such as need of milk, and not of strong meat." As much as to say, indeed it might have been expected of you, that you should have known enough of the Holy Scriptures, to be able to understand and digest such mysteries: but it is not so with you. The apostle speaks of their proficiency in such knowledge as is conveyed by human teaching: as appears by that expression, "When for the time ye ought to be teachers"; which includes not only a practical and experimental, but also a doctrinal knowledge of the truths and mysteries of religion.

Again, the apostle speaks of such knowledge, whereby Christians are enabled to understand things in divinity which are more abstruse and difficult to be understood, and which require great skill in things of this nature. This is more fully expressed in the two next verses: "For every one that useth milk, is unskilful in the word of righteousness: for he is a babe. But strong meat belongeth to them that are of full age, even those who, by reason of use, have their senses exercised to discern both good and evil." It is such knowledge, that proficiency in it shall carry persons beyond the first principles of religion. As here: "Ye have need that one teach you again which be the first principles of the oracles of God." Therefore the apostle, in the beginning of the next chapter, advises them "to leave the first principles of the doctrine of Christ, and to go on unto perfection."

We may observe that the fault of this defect appears, in that they had not made proficiency according to their time. For the time, they ought to have been teachers. As they were Christians, their business was to learn and gain Christian knowledge. They were scholars in the school of Christ; and if they had improved their time in learning, as they ought to have done, they might, by the time when the apostle wrote, have been fit to be teachers in this school. To whatever business any one is devoted, it may be expected that his perfection in it shall be answerable to the time he has had to learn and perfect himself. Christians should not always remain babes, but should grow in Christian knowledge; and leaving the food of babes, they should learn to digest strong meat.

**Doctrine.** Every Christian should make a business of endeavoring to grow in knowledge in divinity. This is indeed esteemed the business of divines and ministers: it is commonly thought to be their work, by the study of the Scriptures, and other instructive books, to gain knowledge; and most seem to think that it may be left to them as what belongeth not to others. But if the apostle had entertained this notion, he would never have blamed the Christian Hebrews for not having acquired knowledge enough to be teachers. Or if he had thought, that this concerned Christians in general only as a thing by the bye, and that their time should not in a considerable measure be taken up with this business; he never would have so much blamed him, that their proficiency in knowledge had not been answerable to the time which they had had to learn.

In handling this subject, I shall show: what is intended by divinity, what kind of knowledge in divinity is intended, why knowledge in divinity is necessary.

And why all Christians should make a business of endeavoring to grow in this knowledge.

## What Is Intended by Divinity
## As the Object of Christian Knowledge

Various definitions have been given of this subject by those who have treated on it. I shall not now stand to inquire which, according to the rules of art, is the most accurate definition; but shall so define or describe it, as I think has the greatest tendency to convey a proper notion of it. It is that science or doctrine which comprehends all those truths and rules which concern the great business of religion.

There are various kinds of arts and sciences taught and learned in the schools, which are conversant about various objects; about the works of nature in general, as philosophy; or the visible heavens, as astronomy; or the sea, as navigation; or the earth, as geography; or the body of man, as physic and anatomy; or the soul of man, with regard to its natural powers and qualities, as logic and pneumatology; or about human government, as politics and jurisprudence. But one science, or kind of knowledge and doctrine, is above all the rest; as it treats concerning God and the great business of religion. Divinity is not learned, as other sciences, merely by the improvement of man's natural reason, but is taught by God Himself in a book full of instruction, which He hath given us for that end. This is the rule which God hath given to the world to be their guide in searching after this kind of knowledge, and is a summary of all things of this nature needful for us to know. Upon this account divinity is rather called a doctrine, than an art or science.

Indeed there is what is called natural religion. There are many truths concerning God, and our duty to him, which are evident by the light of nature. But Christian divinity, properly so called, is not evident by the light of nature; it depends on revelation. Such are our circumstances now in our fallen state, that nothing which it is needful for us to know concerning God, is manifest by the light of nature, in the manner in which it is necessary for us to know it. For the knowledge of no truth in divinity is of significance to us, any otherwise than as it some way or other belongs to the gospel scheme, or as it relates to a mediator. But the light of nature teaches us no truth in this matter. Therefore it cannot be said, that we come to the knowledge of any part of Christian truth by the light of nature. It is only the Word of God, contained in the Old and New Testament, which teaches us Christian divinity.

This comprehends all that is taught in the Scriptures, and so all that we need know, or is to be known, concerning God and Jesus Christ, concerning our duty to God, and our happiness in God. Divinity is commonly defined, the doctrine of living to God; and by some who seem to be more accurate, the doctrine of living to God by Christ. It comprehends all Christian doctrines as they are in Jesus, and all Christian rules directing us in living to God by Christ. There is no one doctrine, no promise, no rule, but what some way or other relates to the Christian and divine life, or our living to God by Christ. They all relate to this, in two respects, viz. as they tend to promote our living to God here in this world, in a life of faith and holiness, and also as they tend to bring us to a life of perfect holiness and happiness, in the full enjoyment of God hereafter.

## What Kind of Knowledge in Divinity Is Intended in the Doctrine

There are two kinds of knowledge of divine truth, viz. speculative and practical, or in other terms, natural and spiritual. The former remains only in the head. No other faculty but the understanding is concerned in it. It consists in having a natural or rational knowledge of the things of religion, or such a knowledge as is to be obtained by the natural exercise of our own faculties, without any special illumination of the Spirit of God. The latter rests not entirely in the head, or in the speculative ideas of things; but the heart is concerned in it: it principally consists in the sense of the heart. The mere intellect, without the will or the inclination, is not the seat of it. And it may not only be called seeing, but feeling or tasting. Thus there is a difference between having a right speculative notion of the doctrines contained in the Word of God, and having a due sense of them in the heart. In the former consists the speculative or natural knowledge; in the latter consists the spiritual or practical knowledge of them.

Neither of these is intended in the doctrine exclusively of the other: but it is intended that we should seek the former in order to the latter. The latter, or the spiritual and practical, is of the greatest importance; for a speculative without a spiritual knowledge, is to no purpose, but to make our condemnation the greater. Yet a speculative knowledge is also of infinite importance in this respect, that without it we can have no spiritual or practical knowledge.

I have already shown, that the apostle speaks not only of a spiritual knowledge, but of such as can be acquired, and communicated from one to another. Yet it is not to be thought, that he means this exclusively of the other. But he would have the Christian Hebrews seek the one, in order to the other. Therefore the former is first and most directly intended; it is intended that Christians should, by reading and other proper means, seek a good rational knowledge of the things of divinity: while the latter is more indirectly intended, since it is to be sought by the other. But I proceed to

## The Usefulness and Necessity of the Knowledge of Divine Truths

There is no other way by which any means of grace whatsoever can be of any benefit, but by knowledge. All teaching is in vain, without learning. Therefore the preaching of the gospel would be wholly to no purpose, if it conveyed no knowledge to the mind. There is an order of men which Christ has appointed on purpose to be teachers in His church. But they teach in vain, if no knowledge in these things is gained by their teaching. It is impossible that their teaching and preaching should be a mean of grace, or of any good in the hearts of their hearers, any otherwise than by knowledge imparted to the understanding. Otherwise it would be of as much benefit to the auditory, if the minister should preach in some unknown tongue. All the difference is, that preaching in a known tongue conveys something to the understanding, which preaching in an unknown tongue does not. On this account, such preaching must be unprofitable. In such things men receive nothing, when they understand nothing; and are not at all edified, unless some knowledge be conveyed; agreeable to the apostle's arguing (I Cor. 14:2–6).

No speech can be a mean of grace but by conveying knowledge. Otherwise the speech is as much lost as if there had been no man there, and if he that spoke, had spoken only into the air; as it follows in the passage just quoted (vv. 6–10). God deals with man as with a rational creature; and when faith is in exercise, it is not about something he knows not what. Therefore hearing is absolutely necessary to faith; because hearing is necessary to understanding (Rom. 10:14). "How they shall believe in him of whom they have not heard?" In like manner, there can be no love without knowledge. It is not according to the nature of the human soul, to love an object which is entirely unknown. The heart cannot be set upon an object of which there is no idea in the understanding. The reasons which induce the soul to love, must first be understood, before they can have a reasonable influence on the heart.

God hath given us the Bible, which is a book of instructions. But this book can be of no manner of profit to us, any otherwise than as it conveys some knowledge to the mind: it can profit us no more than if it were written in the

Chinese or Tartarian language, of which we know not one word. So the sacraments of the gospel can have a proper effect no other way, than by conveying some knowledge. They represent certain things by visible signs. And what is the end of signs, but to convey some knowledge of the things signified? Such is the nature of man, that no object can come at the heart but through the door of the understanding: and there can be no spiritual knowledge of that of which there is not first a rational knowledge. It is impossible that any one should see the truth or excellency of any doctrine of the gospel, who knows not what that doctrine is. A man cannot see the wonderful excellency and love of Christ in doing such and such things for sinners, unless his understanding be first informed how those things were done. He cannot have a taste of the sweetness and excellency of divine truth, unless he first have a notion that there is such a thing.

Without knowledge in divinity, none would differ from the most ignorant and barbarous heathens. The heathens remain in gross darkness because they are not instructed, and have not obtained the knowledge of divine truths.

If men have no knowledge of these things, the faculty of reason in them will be wholly in vain. The faculty of reason and understanding was given for actual understanding and knowledge. If a man have no actual knowledge, the faculty or capacity of knowing is of no use to him. And if he have actual knowledge, yet if he be destitute of the knowledge of those things which are the last end of his being, and for the sake of the knowledge of which he had more understanding given him than the beasts; then still his faculty of reason is in vain; he might as well have been a beast as a man. But divine subjects are the things, to know which we had the faculty of reason given us. They are the things which appertain to the end of our being, and to the great business for which we are made. Therefore a man cannot have his faculty of understanding to any good purpose, further than he hath knowledge of divine truth.

So that this kind of knowledge is absolutely necessary.

Other kinds of knowledge may be very useful. Some other sciences, such as astronomy, natural philosophy, and geography, may be very excellent in their kind. But the knowledge of this divine science is infinitely more useful and important than that of all other sciences whatever.

## Why All Christians Should Make a Business of Endeavoring to Grow in the Knowledge of Divinity

Christians ought not to content themselves with such degrees of knowledge of divinity as they have already obtained. It should not satisfy them, as they know as much as is absolutely necessary to salvation, but they should seek to make progress.

This endeavor to make progress in such knowledge ought not to be attended to as a thing by the bye, but all Christians should make a business of it. They should look upon it as a part of their daily business, and no small part of it neither. It should be attended to as a considerable part of the work of their high calling.—For,

1. Our business should doubtless much consist in employing those faculties, by which we are distinguished from the beasts, about those things which are the main end of those faculties. The reason why we have faculties superior to those of the brutes given us, is, that we are indeed designed for a superior employment. That which the Creator intended should be our main employment, is something above what He intended the beast for, and therefore hath given us superior powers. Therefore, without doubt, it should be a considerable part of our business to improve those superior faculties. But the faculty by which we are chiefly distinguished from the brutes, is the faculty of understanding. It follows then, that we should make it our chief business to improve this faculty, and should by no means prosecute it as a business by the bye. For us to make the improvement of this faculty a business by the bye, is in effect for us to make the faculty of under-

standing itself a "by-faculty," if I may so speak, a faculty of less importance than others: whereas indeed it is the highest faculty we have.

But we cannot make a business of the improvement of our intellectual faculty, any otherwise than by making a business of improving ourselves in actual knowledge. So that those who make not this very much their business; but instead of improving their understanding to acquire knowledge, are chiefly devoted to their inferior power—to please their senses, and gratify their animal appetites—not only behave themselves in a manner not becoming Christians, but also act as if they had forgotten that they are men, and that God hath set them above the brutes, by giving them understanding.

God hath given to man some things in common with the brutes, as his outward senses, his bodily appetites, a capacity of bodily pleasure and pain, and other animal faculties: and some things He hath given him superior to the brutes, the chief of which is a faculty of understanding and reason. Now God never gave man these faculties to be subject to those which he hath in common with the brutes. This would be great confusion, and equivalent to making man to be a servant to the beasts. On the contrary, He has given those inferior powers to be employed in subserviency to man's understanding; and therefore it must be a great part of man's principal business to improve his understanding by acquiring knowledge. If so, then it will follow, that it should be a main part of his business to improve his understanding in acquiring divine knowledge, or the knowledge of the things of divinity: for the knowledge of these things is the principal end of this faculty. God gave man the faculty of understanding, chiefly, that he might understand divine things.

The wiser heathens were sensible that the main business of man was the improvement and exercise of his understanding. But they knew not the object about which the understanding should chiefly be employed. That science which many of them thought should chiefly employ the understanding, was philosophy; and accordingly they made it their chief business to study it. But we who enjoy the light of the gospel are more happy; we are not left, as to this particular, in the dark. God hath told us about what things we should chiefly employ our understandings, having given us a book full of divine instructions, holding forth many glorious objects about which all rational creatures should chiefly employ their understandings. These instructions are accommodated to persons of all capacities and conditions, and proper to be studied, not only by men of learning, but by persons of every character, learned and unlearned, young and old, men and women. Therefore the acquisition of knowledge in these things should be a main business of all those who have the advantage of enjoying the Holy Scriptures.

2. The truths of divinity are of superlative excellency, and are worthy that all should make a business of endeavoring to grow in the knowledge of them. They are as much above those things which are treated of in other sciences, as heaven is above the earth. God Himself, the eternal three in one, is the chief object of this science; and next Jesus Christ, as God-man and Mediator, and the glorious work of redemption, the most glorious work that ever was wrought: then the great things of the heavenly world, the glorious and eternal inheritance purchased by Christ, and promised in the gospel; the work of the Holy Spirit of God on the hearts of men; our duty to God, and the way in which we ourselves may become like angels, and like God Himself in our measure. All these are objects of this science.

Such things as these have been the main subject of the study of the holy patriarchs, prophets, and apostles, and the most excellent men that ever existed; and they are also the subject of study to the angels in heaven (I Peter 1:10–12). They are so excellent and worthy to be known, that the knowledge of them will richly pay for all the pains and labor of an earnest seeking of it. If there were a great treasure of gold and pearls accidentally found, and opened with such circumstances that all might have as much as they could gather; would not every one think it worth his while to make a business of gathering while it should last? But that treasure of divine knowledge, which is contained in the Scriptures, and is provided for every one to gather to himself as much of it as he can, is far more rich than any one of gold and pearls. How busy are all sorts of men, all over the world, in getting riches? But this knowledge is a far better kind of riches, than that after which they so diligently and laboriously pursue.

3. Divine truths not only concern ministers, but are of infinite importance to all Christians. It is not with the doctrines of divinity as it is with the doctrines of philosophy and other sciences. These last are generally speculative points, which are of little concern in human life; and it very little alters the case as to our temporal or spiritual interests, whether we know them or not. Philosophers differ about them, some being of one opinion, and others of another. And while they are engaged in warm disputes about them, others may well leave them to dispute among themselves, without troubling their heads much about them; it being of little concern to them whether the one or the other be in the right. But it is not thus in matters of divinity. The doctrines of this nearly concern every one. They are about those things which relate to every man's eternal salvation and happiness. The common people cannot say, Let us leave these matters to ministers and divines; let them dispute them out among themselves as they can; they concern not us: for they are of infinite importance to every man. Those doctrines which relate to the essence, attributes, and subsistencies of God, concern all; as it is of infinite importance to common people, as well as to ministers, to know what kind of being God is. For He is a being who hath made us all, "in whom we live, and move, and have our being"; who is the Lord of all; the being to whom we are all accountable; is the last end of our being, and the only fountain of our happiness.

The doctrines also which relate to Jesus Christ and His

mediation, His incarnation, His life and death, His resurrection and ascension, His sitting at the right hand of the Father, His satisfaction and intercession, infinitely concern common people as well as divines. They stand in as much need of this Savior, and of an interest in His person and offices, and the things which He hath done and suffered, as ministers and divines. The same may be said of the doctrines which relate to the manner of a sinner's justification, or the way in which he becomes interested in the mediation of Christ. They equally concern all; for all stand in equal necessity of justification before God. That eternal condemnation, to which we are all naturally exposed, is equally dreadful. So with respect to those doctrines which relate to the work of the Spirit of God on the heart, in the application of redemption in our effectual calling and sanctification, all are equally concerned in them. There is no doctrine of divinity whatever, which doth not some way or other concern the eternal interest of every Christian.

4. We may argue in favor of the same position, from the great things which God hath done in order to give us instruction in these things. As to other sciences, He hath left us to ourselves, to the light of our own reason. But divine things being of infinitely greater importance to us, He hath not left us to an uncertain guide; but hath Himself given us a revelation of the truth in these matters, and hath done very great things to convey and confirm it to us; raising up many prophets in different ages, immediately inspiring them with His Holy Spirit, and confirming their doctrine with innumerable miracles or wonderful works out of the "established" course of nature. Yea, He raised up a succession of prophets, which was upheld for several ages.

It was very much for this end that God separated the people of Israel, in so wonderful a manner, from all other people, and kept them separate; that to them He might commit the oracles of God, and that from them they might be communicated to the world. He hath also often sent angels to bring divine instructions to men; and hath often

Himself appeared in miraculous symbols or repre-
sentations of His presence: and now in these last days hath
sent His own Son into the world, to be His great prophet,
to teach us divine truth (Heb. 1:1 ff.). God hath given us a
book of divine instructions, which contains the sum of divinity. Now, these things hath God done, not only for the
instruction of ministers and men of learning; but for the
instruction of all men, of all sorts, learned and unlearned,
men, women, and children. And certainly if God doth
such great things to teach us, we ought to do something to
learn.

God giving instructions to men in these things, is not a
business by the bye; but what He hath undertaken and
prosecuted in a course of great and wonderful dis-
pensations, as an affair in which His heart hath been
greatly engaged; which is sometimes in Scripture signified
by the expression of God's rising early to teach us, and to
send us prophets and teachers (Jer. 7:25). "Since that day
that your fathers came forth out of the land of Egypt, unto
this day, I have even sent unto you all my servants the
prophets, daily rising up early, and sending them." And
verse 13: "I spake unto you, rising up early and speaking."
This is a figurative speech, signifying that God hath done
this as a business of great importance, in which He took
great care, and had His heart much engaged; because persons are wont to rise early to prosecute such business as
they are earnestly engaged in. If God hath been so engaged in teaching, certainly we should not be negligent in
learning; but should make growing in knowledge a great
part of the business of our lives.

5. It may be argued from the abundance of the instructions which God hath given us, from the largeness of that
book which God hath given to teach us divinity, and from
the great variety that is therein contained. Much was
taught by Moses of old, which we have transmitted down
to us; after that, other books were from time to time
added; much is taught us by David and Solomon; and
many and excellent are the instructions communicated by

the prophets: yet God did not think all this enough, but after this sent Christ and His apostles, by whom there is added a great and excellent treasure to that holy book, which is to be our rule in the study of this important subject.

This book was written for the use of all; all are directed to search the Scriptures (John 5:39). "Search the scriptures, that testify of me"; and Isaiah 34:16: "Seek ye out of the book of the Lord, and read." They that read and understand are pronounced blessed (Rev. 1:3). "Blessed is he that readeth, and they that understand the words of this prophecy." If this be true of that particular book of the Revelation, much more is it true of the Bible in general. Nor is it to be believed that God would have given instructions in such abundance, if He had intended that receiving instruction should be only a bye concern with us.

It is to be considered, that all those abundant instructions which are contained in the Scriptures were written that they might be understood; otherwise they are not instructions. That which is not given that the learner may understand it, is not given for the learner's instruction: and unless we endeavor to grow in the knowledge of divinity, a very great part of those instructions will to us be in vain; for we can receive benefit by no more of the Scriptures than we understand. We have reason to bless God that He hath given us such various and plentiful instruction in His Word; but we shall be hypocritical in so doing, if we after all content ourselves with but little of this instruction.

When God hath opened a very large treasure before us, for the supply of our wants, and we thank Him that He hath given us so much; if at the same time we be willing to remain destitute of the greatest part of it, because we are too lazy to gather it, this will not show the sincerity of our thankfulness. We are now under much greater advantages to acquire knowledge in divinity, than the people of God were of old, because since that time the canon of Scripture is much increased. But if we be negligent of our advantages, we may be never the better for them, and may remain with as little knowledge as they.

6. However diligently we apply ourselves, there is room enough to increase our knowledge in divine truth. None have this excuse to make for not diligently applying themselves to gain knowledge in divinity, that they already know all; nor can they make this excuse, that they have no need diligently to apply themselves, in order to know all that is to be known. None can excuse themselves for want of business in which to employ themselves. There is room enough to employ ourselves for ever in this divine science, with the utmost application. Those who have applied themselves most closely, have studied the longest, and have made the greatest attainments in this knowledge, know but little of what is to be known. The subject is inexhaustible. That divine being, who is the main subject of this science, is infinite, and there is no end to the glory of His perfections. His works at the same time are wonderful, and cannot be found out to perfection; especially the work of redemption, about which the science of divinity is chiefly conversant, is full of unsearchable wonders.

The Word of God, which is given for our instruction in divinity, contains enough in it to employ us to the end of our lives, and then we shall leave enough uninvestigated to employ the heads of the ablest divines to the end of the world. The psalmist found an end to the things that are human; but he could never find an end to what is contained in the Word of God (Ps. 119:96). "I have seen an end of all perfection; but thy command is exceeding broad." There is enough in this divine science to employ the understandings of saints and angels to all eternity.

7. It doubtless concerns every one to endeavor to excel in the knowledge of things which pertain to his profession, or principal calling. If it concerns men to excel in any thing, or in any wisdom or knowledge at all, it certainly concerns them to excel in the affairs of their main profession and work. But the calling and work of every Christian is to live to God. This is said to be his high calling (Phil.

3:14). This is the business, and, if I may so speak, the trade of a Christian, his main work, and indeed should be his only work. No business should be done by a Christian, but as it is some way or other a part of this. Therefore certainly the Christian should endeavor to be well acquainted with those things which belong to this work, that he may fulfill it, and be thoroughly furnished to it.

It becomes one who is called to be a soldier, to excel in the art of war. It becomes a mariner to excel in the art of navigation. It becomes a physician to excel in the knowledge of those things which pertain to the art of physic. So it becomes all such as profess to be Christians, and to devote themselves to the practice of Christianity, to endeavor to excel in the knowledge of divinity.

8. It may be argued hence, that God hath appointed an order of men for this end, to assist persons in gaining knowledge in these things. He hath appointed them to be teachers (I Cor. 12:28); and God hath set some in the church; first apostles, secondarily prophets, thirdly teachers (Eph. 4:11–12). "He gave some apostles; some, prophets, some, evangelists; some, pastors and teachers; for the perfecting of the saints, for the work of the ministry, for the edifying of the body of Christ." If God hath set them to be teachers, making that their business, then He hath made it their business to impart knowledge. But what kind of knowledge? Not the knowledge of philosophy, or of human laws, or of mechanical arts, but of divinity.

If God hath made it the business of some to be teachers, it will follow, that He hath made it the business of others to be learners; for teachers and learners are correlates, one of which was never intended to be without the other. God hath never made it the duty of some to take pains to teach those who are not obliged to take pains to learn. He hath not commanded ministers to spend themselves, in order to impart knowledge to those who are not obliged to apply themselves to receive it.

The name by which Christians are commonly called in the New Testament is "disciples," the signification of which word is scholars or learners. All Christians are put into the school of Christ, where their business is to learn, or receive knowledge from Christ, their common master and teacher, and from those inferior teachers appointed by Him to instruct in His name.

9. God hath in the Scriptures plainly revealed it to be His will, that all Christians should diligently endeavor to excel in the knowledge of divine things. It is the revealed will of God, that Christians should not only have some knowledge of things of this nature, but that they should be enriched with all knowledge (I Cor. 1:4–5). "I thank my God always on your behalf, for the grace of God that is given you by Jesus Christ, that in every thing ye are enriched by him, in all utterance, and in all knowledge." So the apostle earnestly prayed, that the Christian Philippians might abound more and more, not only in love, but in Christian knowledge (Phil. 1:9). "And this I pray, that your love may abound yet more and more in knowledge, and in all judgment." So the apostle Peter advises to "give all diligence to add to faith virtue, and to virtue knowledge" (II Peter 1:5); and the apostle Paul, in the next chapter to that wherein is the text, counsels the Christian Hebrews, leaving the first principles of the doctrine of Christ, to go on to perfection. He would by no means have them always to rest only in those fundamental doctrines of repentance, and faith, and the resurrection from the dead, and the eternal judgment, in which they were instructed when baptized, at their first initiation in Christianity (see Heb. 6).

## An Exhortation That All May Diligently Endeavor to Gain Christian Knowledge

Consider yourselves as scholars or disciples, put into the school of Christ; and therefore be diligent to make proficiency in Christian knowledge. Content not yourselves with this, that you have been taught your catechism in your childhood, and that you know as much of the principles of religion as is necessary to salvation; else you will be guilty of what the apostle warns against, viz. going no further than laying the foundation of repentance from dead works, etc.

You are all called to be Christians, and this is your profession. Endeavor, therefore, to acquire knowledge in things which pertain to your profession. Let not your teachers have cause to complain, that while they spend and are spent, to impart knowledge to you, you take little pains to learn. It is a great encouragement to an instructor, to have such to teach as make a business of learning, bending their minds to it. This makes teaching a pleasure, when otherwise it will be a very heavy and burdensome task.

You all have by you a large treasure of divine knowledge, in that you have the Bible in your hands; therefore be not contented in possessing but little of this treasure. God hath spoken much to you in the Scriptures; labor to understand as much of what He saith as you can. God hath made you all reasonable creatures; therefore let not the noble faculty of reason or understanding lie neglected. Content not yourselves with having so much knowledge as is thrown in your way, and received in some sense unavoidably by the frequent inculcation of divine truth in the preaching of the Word, of which you are obliged to be hearers, or accidentally gain in conversation; but let it be very much your business to search for it, and that with the same diligence and labor with which men are wont to dig in mines of silver and gold.

Especially I would advise those who are young to employ themselves in this way. Men are never too old to learn; but the time of youth is especially the time for learning; it is peculiarly proper for gaining and storing up knowledge. Further, to stir up all, both old and young, to this duty, let me entreat you to consider:

1. If you apply yourselves diligently to this work, you will not want employment, when you are at leisure from your common secular business. In this way, you may find

something in which you may profitably employ yourselves. You will find something else to do, besides going about from house to house, spending one hour after another in unprofitable conversation, or, at best, to no other purpose but to amuse yourselves, to fill up and wear away your time. And it is to be feared that very much of the time spent in evening visits, is spent to a much worse purpose than that which I have now mentioned. Solomon tells us (Prov. 10:19), "That in the multitude of words, there wanteth not sin." And is not this verified in those who find little else to do but to go to one another's house, and spend the time in such talk as comes next, or such as any one's present disposition happens to suggest?

Some diversion is doubtless lawful; but for Christians to spend so much of their time, so many long evenings, in no other conversation than that which tends to divert and amuse, if nothing worse, is a sinful way of spending time, and tends to poverty of soul at least, if not to outward poverty (Prov. 14:23). "In all labour there is profit; but the talk of the lips tendeth only to penury." Besides, when persons for so much of their time have nothing else to do, but to sit, and talk, and chat, there is great danger of falling into foolish and sinful conversation, venting their corrupt dispositions, in talking against others, expressing their jealousies and evil surmises concerning their neighbors; not considering what Christ hath said (Matt. 12:36). "Of every idle word that men shall speak, shall they give account in the day of judgment."

If you would comply with what you have heard from this doctrine, you would find something else to employ your time besides contention, or talking about those public affairs which tend to contention. Young people might find something else to do, besides spending their time in vain company; something that would be much more profitable to themselves, as it would really turn to some good account; something in doing which they would both be more out of the way of temptation, and be more in the way of duty, and of a divine blessing. And even aged people would have something to employ themselves in, after they are become incapable of bodily labor. Their time, as is now often the case, would not lie heavy upon their hands, as they would with both profit and pleasure be engaged in searching the Scriptures, and in comparing and meditating upon the various truths which they should find there.

2. This would be a noble way of spending your time. The Holy Spirit gives the Bereans this epithet, because they diligently employed themselves in this business (Acts 17:11). "These were more noble than those of Thessalonica in that they received the word with all readiness of mind, and searched the scriptures daily, whether those things were so." Similar to this is very much the employment of heaven. The inhabitants of that world spend much of their time in searching into the great things of divinity, and endeavoring to acquire knowledge in them, as we are told of the angels (I Peter 1:12). "Which things the angels desire to look into." This will be very agreeable to what you hope will be your business to all eternity, as you doubtless hope to join in the same employment with the angels of light. Solomon says (Prov. 25:2), "It is the honor of kings to search out a matter"; and certainly, above all others, to search out divine matters. Now, if this be the honor even of kings, is it not equally if not much more your honor?

3. This is a pleasant way of improving time. Knowledge is pleasant and delightful to intelligent creatures, and above all, the knowledge of divine things; for in them are the most excellent truths, and the most beautiful and amiable objects held forth to view. However tedious the labor necessarily attending this business may be, yet the knowledge once obtained will richly requite the pains taken to obtain it. "When wisdom entereth the heart, knowledge is pleasant to the soul" (Prov. 2:10).

4. This knowledge is exceeding useful in Christian practice. Such as have much knowledge in divinity have great means and advantages for spiritual and saving knowledge; for no means of grace have a saving effect,

otherwise than by the knowledge they impart. The more you have of a rational knowledge of divine things, the more opportunity will there be, when the Spirit shall be breathed into your heart, to see the excellency of these things, and to taste the sweetness of them. The heathens, who have no rational knowledge of the things of the gospel, have no opportunity to see the excellency of them; and therefore the more rational knowledge of these things you have, the more opportunity and advantage you have to see the divine excellency and glory of them.

Again, the more knowledge you have of divine things, the better will you know your duty; your knowledge will be of great use to direct you as to your duty in particular cases. You will also be the better furnished against the temptations of the devil. For the devil also takes advantage of persons' ignorance to ply them with temptations which otherwise would have no hold of them. By having much knowledge, you will be under greater advantages to conduct yourselves with prudence and discretion in your Christian course, and so to live much more to the honor of God and religion. Many who mean well, and are full of a good spirit, yet for want of prudence, conduct themselves so as to wound religion. Many have a zeal of God, which does more hurt than good, because it is not according to knowledge (Rom 10:2). The reason why many good men behave no better in many instances, is not so much that they want grace, as that they want knowledge. Beside, an increase of knowledge would be a great help to profitable conversation. It would supply you with matter for conversation when you come together, or when you visit your neighbors: and so you would have less temptation to spend the time in such conversation as tends to your own and others' hurt.

5. Consider the advantages you are under to grow in the knowledge of divinity. We are under far greater advantages to gain much of this knowledge now, than God's people under the Old Testament, both because the canon of Scripture is so much enlarged since that time, and also

because evangelical truths are now so much more plainly revealed. So that common men are now in some respects under advantages to know more, than the greatest prophets were then. Thus that saying of Christ is in a sense applicable to us (Luke 10:23–24), "Blessed are the eyes which see the things which ye see. For I tell you, that many prophets and kings have desired to see those things which ye see, and have not seen them; and to hear those things which ye hear, and have not heard them." We are in some respects under far greater advantages for gaining knowledge, now in these latter ages of the church, than Christians were formerly; especially by reason of the art of printing, of which God hath given us the benefit, whereby Bibles and other books of divinity are exceedingly multiplied, and persons may now be furnished with helps for the obtaining of Christian knowledge, at a much easier and cheaper rate than they formerly could.

6. We know not what opposition we may meet within the religious principles which we hold. We know that there are many adversaries to the gospel and its truths. If therefore we embrace those truths, we must expect to be attacked by the said adversaries; and unless we be well informed concerning divine things, how shall we be able to defend ourselves? Beside, the apostle Peter enjoins it upon us, always to be ready to give an answer to every man who asketh us a reason of the hope that is in us. But this we cannot expect to do without considerable knowledge in divine things.

## Directions for the Acquisition of Christian Knowledge

1. Be assiduous in reading the Holy Scriptures. This is the fountain whence all knowledge in divinity must be derived. Therefore let not this treasure lie by you neglected. Every man of common understanding who can read, may, if he please, become well acquainted with the Scriptures. And what an excellent attainment would this be!

2. Content not yourselves with only a cursory reading without regarding the sense. This is an ill way of reading, to which, however, many accustom themselves all their days. When you read, observe what you read. Observe how things come in. Take notice of the drift of the discourse, and compare one Scripture with another. For the Scripture, by the harmony of its different parts, casts great light upon itself. We are expressly directed by Christ, to search the Scriptures, which evidently intends something more than a mere cursory reading. And use means to find out the meaning of the Scripture. When you have it explained in the preaching of the Word, take notice of it; and if at any time a Scripture that you did not understand be cleared up to your satisfaction, mark it, lay it up, and if possible remember it.

3. Procure, and diligently use, other books which may help you to grow in this knowledge. There are many excellent books extant, which might greatly forward you in this knowledge, and afford you a very profitable and pleasant entertainment in your leisure hours. There is doubtless a great defect in many, that through a loathness to be at a little expense, they furnish themselves with no more helps of this nature. They have a few books indeed, which now and then on Sabbath-days they read; but they have had them so long, and read them so often, that they are weary of them, and it is now become a dull story, a mere task to read them.

4. Improve conversation with others to this end. How much might persons promote each other's knowledge in divine things, if they would improve conversation as they might; if men that are ignorant were not ashamed to show their ignorance, and were willing to learn of others; if those that have knowledge would communicate it, without pride and ostentation; and if all were more disposed to enter on such conversation as would be for their mutual edification and instruction.

5. Seek not to grow in knowledge chiefly for the sake of applause, and to enable you to dispute with others; but

seek it for the benefit of your souls, and in order to practice. If applause be your end, you will not be so likely to be
led to the knowledge of the truth, but may justly, as often
is the case of those who are proud of their knowledge, be
led into error to your own perdition. This being your end,
if you should obtain much rational knowledge, it would
not be likely to be of any benefit to you, but would puff
you up with pride (I Cor. 8:1). "Knowledge puffeth up."

6. Seek to God, that he would direct you, and bless you,
in this pursuit after knowledge. This is the apostle's direction (James 1:5). "If any man lack wisdom, let him ask it of
God, who giveth to all liberally, and upbraideth not." God
is the fountain of all divine knowledge (Prov. 2:6). "The
Lord giveth wisdom: out of his mouth cometh knowledge
and understanding." Labor to be sensible of your own
blindness and ignorance, and your need of the help of
God, lest you be led into error, instead of true knowledge
(I Cor. 3:18). "If any man would be wise, let him become a
fool, that he may be wise."

7. Practice according to what knowledge you have. This
will be the way to know more. The psalmist warmly recommends this way of seeking knowledge in divine truth,
from his own experience (Ps. 119:100). "I understand
more than the ancients, because I keep thy precepts."
Christ also recommends the same (John 7:17). "If any man
will do his will, he shall know of the doctrine, whether it be
of God, or whether I speak of myself."

From *The Works of President Edwards,* vol. v, by Jonathan Edwards.

*B. B. Warfield*

# 10

# The Idea of
# Systematic Theology

The term "systematic theology" has long been in some-what general use, especially in America, to designate one of the theological disciplines. And, on the whole, it appears to be a sufficiently exact designation of this discipline. It has not, of course, escaped criticism. The main faults that have been found with it are succinctly summed up by a recent writer in the following compact phrases:

> The expression "systematic theology" is really an imper-tinent tautology. It is a tautology, in so far as a theology that is not systematic or methodical would be no theology. The idea of rational method lies in the word *logos,* which forms part of the term theology. And it is an impertinence, in so far as it suggests that there are other theological dis-ciplinae, or departments of theology, which are not methodical.[1]

Is not this, however, just a shade hypercritical? What is meant by calling this discipline "systematic theology" is not that it deals with its material in a systematic or methodical way, and the other disciplines do not; but that it presents its material in the form of a system. Other disciplines may use a chronological, a historical, or some other method: this discipline must needs employ a systematic, that is to say, a philosophical or scientific method. It might be equally well designated, therefore, "philosophical theol-ogy," or "scientific theology." But we should not by the adoption of one of these terms escape the ambiguities which are charged against the term "systematic theology." Other theological disciplines may also claim to be philosophical or scientific. If exegesis should be systematic, it should also be scientific. If history should be methodical, it should also be philosophical. An additional ambiguity would also be brought to these terms from their popular usage. There would be danger that "philosophical theology" should be misapprehended as theology dominated by some philosophical system. There would be a similar danger that "scientific theology" should be misunderstood as theology reduced to an empirical science, or dependent upon an "experimental method." Nevertheless these terms also would fairly describe what we mean by "systematic theology." They too would discriminate it from its sister disciplines, as the philosophical discipline which investigates from the philosophical standpoint the matter with which all the disciplines deal. And they would keep clearly before our minds the main fact in the case, namely, that systematic theology, as distinguished from its sister disciplines, is a science, and is to be conceived as a science and treated as a science.

The two designations, "philosophical theology" and "scientific theology," are practically synonyms. But they differ in their connotation as the terms "philosophy" and "science" differ. The distinction between these terms in a reference like the present would seem to be that between the whole and one of its parts. Philosophy is the *scientia scientiarum*. What a science does for a division of knowledge, that philosophy essays to do for the mass of knowledge. A science reduces a section of our knowledge to order and harmony: philosophy reduces the sciences to order and harmony. Accordingly there are many sciences, and but one philosophy. We, therefore, so far agree with Professor D. W. Simon (whom we have quoted above in order to disagree with him), when he says that "what a science properly understood does for a subsystem; that, philosophy aims to do for the system which the subsystems constitute." "Its function is so to grasp the whole that every part shall find its proper place therein, and the parts, that they shall form an orderly organic whole": "so to correlate the *reals,* which with their interactivities make up the world or the universe, that the whole shall be seen in its harmony and unity; and that to every individual real shall be assigned the place in which it can be seen to be discharging its proper functions."[2] This, as will be at once perceived, is the function of each science in its own sphere. To call "systematic theology" "philosophical theology" or "scientific theology" would therefore be all one in essential meaning. Only, when we call it "philosophical theology," we should be conceiving it as a science among the sciences and should have our eye upon its place in the universal sum of knowledge: while, when we call it "scientific theology," our mind should be occupied with it in itself, as it were in isolation, and with the proper mode of dealing with its material. In either case we are affirming that it deals with its material as an organizable system of knowledge; that it deals with it from the philosophical point of view; that it is, in other words, in its essential nature a science.

It is possible that the implications of this determination are not always fully realized. When we have made the simple assertion of "systematic theology" that it is in its essential nature a science, we have already determined most of the vexing questions which arise concerning it in a formal point of view. In this single predicate is implicitly included a series of affirmations, which, when taken together, will give us a rather clear conception not only of what systematic theology is, but also of what it deals with, whence it obtains its material, and for what purpose it exists.

1. First of all, then, let us observe that to say that systematic theology is a science is to deny that it is a historical discipline, and to affirm that it seeks to discover, not what has been or is held to be true, but what is ideally true; in other words, it is to declare that it deals with absolute truth and aims at organizing into a concatenated system all the

truth in its sphere. Geology is a science, and on that very account there cannot be two geologies; its matter is all the well-authenticated facts in its sphere, and its aim is to digest all these facts into one all-comprehending system. There may be rival psychologies, which fill the world with vain jangling; but they do not strive together in order that they may obtain the right to exist side by side in equal validity, but in strenuous effort to supplant and supersede one another: there can be but one true science of mind. In like manner, just because theology is a science there can be but one theology. This all-embracing system will brook no rival in its sphere, and there can be two theologies only at the cost of one or both of them being imperfect, incomplete, false. It is because theology, in accordance with a somewhat prevalent point of view, is often looked upon as a historical rather than a scientific discipline, that it is so frequently spoken of and defined as if it were but one of many similar schemes of thought. There is no doubt such a thing as Christian theology, as distinguished from Buddhist theology or Mohammedan theology; and men may study it as the theological implication of Christianity considered as one of the world's religions. But when studied from this point of view, it forms a section of a historical discipline and furnishes its share of facts for a history of religions; on the data supplied by which a science or philosophy of religion may in turn be based. We may also, no doubt, speak of the Pelagian and Augustinian theologies, or of the Calvinistic and Arminian theologies; but, again, we are speaking as historians and from a historical point of view. The Pelagian and Augustinian theologies are not two coördinate sciences of theology; they are rival theologies. If one is true, just so far the other is false, and there is but one theology. This we may identify, as an empirical fact, with either or neither; but it is at all events one, inclusive of all theological truth and exclusive of all else as false or not germane to the subject.

In asserting that theology is a science, then, we assert that, in its subject matter, it includes all the facts belonging to that sphere of truth which we call theological; and we deny that it needs or will admit of limitation by a discriminating adjectival definition. We may speak of it as Christian theology just as we may speak of it as true theology, if we mean thereby only more fully to describe what, as a matter of fact, theology is found to be; but not, if we mean thereby to discriminate it from some other assumed theology thus erected to a coördinate position with it. We may describe our method of procedure in attempting to ascertain and organize the truths that come before us for building into the system, and so speak of logical or inductive, of speculative or organic theology; or we may separate the one body of theology into its members, and, just as we speak of surface and organic geology or of physiological and direct psychology, so speak of the theology of grace and of sin, or of natural and revealed theology. But all these are but designations of methods of procedure in dealing with the one whole, or of the various sections that together constitute the one whole, which in its completeness is the science of theology, and which, as a science, is inclusive of all the truth in its sphere, however ascertained, however presented, however defined.

2. There is much more than this included, however, in calling theology a science. For the very existence of any science, three things are presupposed: (1) the reality of its subject matter; (2) the capacity of the human mind to apprehend, receive into itself, and rationalize this subject matter; and (3) some medium of communication by which the subject matter is brought before the mind and presented to it for apprehension. There could be no astronomy, for example, if there were no heavenly bodies. And though the heavenly bodies existed, there could still be no science of them were there no mind to apprehend them. Facts do not make a science; they must be not only apprehended, but also so far comprehended as to be rationalized and thus combined into a correlated system. The mind brings to every science somewhat which, though included in the facts, is not derived from the facts consid-

ered in themselves alone, as isolated data; or even as data perceived in some sort of relation to one another. Though they be thus known, science is not yet; and is not born save through the efforts of the mind in subsuming the facts under its own intuitions and forms of thought. No mind is satisfied with a bare cognition of facts; its very constitution forces it on to a restless energy until it succeeds in working these facts not only into a network of correlated relations among themselves, but also into a rational body of thought correlated to itself and its necessary modes of thinking. The condition of science, then, is that the facts which fall within its scope shall be such as stand in relation not only to our faculties, so that they may be apprehended; but also to our mental constitution so that they may be so far understood as to be rationalized and wrought into a system relative to our thinking. Thus a science of aesthetics presupposes an aesthetic faculty, and a science of morals a moral nature, as truly as a science of logic presupposes a logical apprehension, and a science of mathematics a capacity to comprehend the relations of numbers. But still again, though the facts had real existence, and the mind were furnished with a capacity for their reception and for a sympathetic estimate and embracing of them in their relations, no science could exist were there no media by which the facts should be brought before and communicated to the mind. The transmitter and intermediating wire are as essential for telegraphing as the message and the receiving instrument. Subjectively speaking, sense perception is the essential basis of all science of external things; self-consciousness, of internal things. But objective media are also necessary. For example, there could be no astronomy, were there no trembling ether through whose delicate telegraphy the facts of light and heat are transmitted to us from the suns and systems of the heavens. Subjective and objective conditions of communication must unite, before the facts that constitute the material of a science can be placed before the mind that gives it its form. The sense of sight is essential to astronomy: yet the sense of sight would be useless for forming an astronomy were there no objective ethereal messengers to bring us news from the stars. With these an astronomy becomes possible; but how meager an astonomy compared with the new possibilities which have opened out with the discovery of a new medium of communication in the telescope, followed by still newer media in the subtle instruments by which our modern investigators not only weigh the spheres in their courses, but analyze them into their chemical elements, map out the heavens in a chart, and separate the suns into their primary constituents.

Like all other sciences, therefore, theology, for its very existence as a science, presupposes the objective reality of the subject matter with which it deals; the subjective capacity of the human mind so far to understand this subject matter as to be able to subsume it under the firms of its thinking and to rationalize it into not only a comprehensive, but also a comprehensible whole; and the existence of trustworthy media of communication by which the subject matter is brought to the mind and presented before it for perception and understanding. That is to say: (1) The affirmation that theology is a science presupposes the affirmation that God is, and that He has relation to His creatures. Were there no God, there could be no theology; nor could there be a theology if, though He existed, He existed out of relation with His creatures. The whole body of philosophical apologetics is, therefore, presupposed in and underlies the structure of scientific theology. (2) The affirmation that theology is a science presupposes the affirmation that man has a religious nature, that is, a nature capable of understanding not only that God is, but also, to some extent, what he is; not only that He stands in relations with His creatures, but also what those relations are. Had man no religious nature he might, indeed, apprehend certain facts concerning God, but he could not so understand Him in His relations to man as to be able to respond to those facts in a true and sympathetic embrace. The total product of the great science of religion, which investigates the nature and workings of this element in man's mental constitution, is therefore presupposed in and underlies the structure of scientific theology. (3) The affirmation that theology is a science presupposes the affirmation that there are media of communication by which God and divine things are brought before the minds of men, that they may perceive them and, in perceiving, understand them. In other words, when we affirm that theology is a science, we affirm not only the reality of God's existence and our capacity so far to understand Him, but we affirm that He has made Himself known to us—we affirm the objective reality of a revelation. Were there no revelation of God to man, our capacity to understand Him would lie dormant and unawakened; and though He really existed it would be to us as if He were not. There would be a God to be known and a mind to know Him; but theology would be as impossible as if there were neither the one nor the other. Not only, then, philosophical, but also the whole mass of historical apologetics by which the reality of revelation and its embodiment in the Scriptures are vindicated, is presupposed in and underlies the structure of scientific theology.

3. In thus developing the implications of calling theology a science, we have already gone far towards determining our exact conception of what theology is. We have in effect, for example, settled our definition of theology. A science is defined from its subject matter; and the subject matter of theology is God in His Nature and in His relations with His creatures. Theology is therefore that science which treats of God and of the relations between God and the universe. To this definition most theologians have actually come. And those who define theology as "the science of God," mean the term God in a broad sense as inclusive also of His relations; while others exhibit their sense of the need of this inclusiveness by calling it "the

science of God and of divine things"; while still others speak of it, more loosely, as "the science of the super-natural." These definitions fail rather in precision of language than in correctness of conception.

Others, however, go astray in the conception itself. Thus theologians of the school of Schleiermacher usually derive their definition from the sources rather than the subject matter of the science—and so speak of theology as "the science of faith" or the like; a thoroughly unscientific procedure, even though our view of the sources be complete and unexceptionable, which is certainly not the case with this school. Quite as confusing is it to define theology, as is very currently done and often as an outgrowth of this same subjective tendency, as "the science of religions," or even—pressing to its greatest extreme the historical conception, which as often underlies this type of definition—as "the science of the Christian religion." Theology and religion are parallel products of the same body of facts in diverse spheres; the one in the sphere of thought and the other in the sphere of life. And the definition of theology as "the science of religion" thus confounds the product of the facts concerning God and His relations with His creatures working through the hearts and lives of men, with those facts themselves; and consequently, whenever strictly understood, bases theology not on the facts of the divine revelation, but on the facts of the religious life. This leads ultimately to a confusion of the two distinct disciplines of theology, the subject matter of which is objective, and the science of religion, the subject matter of which is subjective; with the effect of lowering the data of theology to the level of the aspirations and imaginings of man's own heart. Wherever this definition is found, either a subjective conception of theology, which reduces it to a branch of psychology, may be suspected; or else a historical conception of it, a conception of "Christian theology" as one of the many theologies of the world, parallel with, even if unspeakably truer than, the others with which it is classed and in conjunction with which it furnishes us with a full account of religion. When so conceived, it is natural to take a step further and permit the methodology of the science, as well as its idea, to be determined by its distinguishing element: thus theology, in contradiction to its very name, becomes Christocentric. No doubt "Christian theology," as a historical discipline, is Christocentric; it is by its doctrine of redemption that it is differentiated from all the other theologies that the world has known. But theology as a science is and must be theocentric. So soon as we firmly grasp it from the scientific point of view, we see that there can be but one science of God and of His relations to His universe, and we no longer seek a point of discrimination, but rather a center of development; and we quickly see that there can be but one center about which so comprehensive a subject matter can be organized—the conception of God. He that hath seen Christ, has beyond doubt seen the Father; but it is one thing to make Christ the center of theology so far as He is one with God, and another thing to organize all theology around Him as the theanthropos and in His specifically theanthropic work.

4. Not only, however, is our definition of theology thus set for us: we have also determined in advance our conception of its sources. We have already made use of the term "revelation," to designate the medium by which the facts concerning God and His relations to His creatures are brought before men's minds, and so made the subject matter of a possible science. The word accurately describes the condition of all knowledge of God. If God be a person, it follows by stringent necessity, that He can be known only so far as He reveals or expresses Himself. And it is but the converse of this, that if there be no revelation, there can be no knowledge, and, of course, no systematized knowledge or science of God. Our reaching up to Him in thought and inference is possible only because He condescends to make Himself intelligible to us, to speak to us through work or word, to reveal Himself. We hazard nothing, therefore, in

saying that, as the condition of all theology is a revealed God, so, without limitation, the sole source of theology is revelation.

In so speaking, however, we have no thought of doubting that God's revelation of Himself is "in divers manners." We have no desire to deny that He has never left man without witness of His eternal power and Godhead, or that He has multiplied the manifestations of Himself in nature and providence and grace, so that every generation has had abiding and unmistakable evidence that He is, that He is the good God, and that He is a God who marketh iniquity. Under the broad skirts of the term "revelation," every method of manifesting Himself which God uses in communicating knowledge of His being and attributes, may find shelter for itself—whether it be through those visible things of nature whereby His invisible things are clearly seen, or through the constitution of the human mind with its casual judgment indelibly stamped upon it, or through that voice of God that we call conscience, which proclaims His moral law within us, or through His providence in which He makes bare His arm for the government of the nations, or through the exercises of His grace, our experience under the tutelage of the Holy Ghost—or whether it be through the open visions of His prophets, the divinely-breathed pages of His written Word, the divine life of the Word Himself. How God reveals Himself—in what divers manners He makes Himself known to His creatures—is thus the subsequent question, by raising which we distribute the one source of theology, revelation, into the various methods of revelation, each of which brings us true knowledge of God, and all of which must be taken account of in building our knowledge into one all-comprehending system. It is the accepted method of theology to infer that the God that made the eye must Himself see; that the God who sovereignly distributes His favors in the secular world may be sovereign in grace too; that the heart that condemns itself but repeats the condemnation of the greater God; that the songs of joy in which the Christian's happy soul voices its sense of God's gratuitous mercy are valid evidence that God has really dealt graciously with it. It is with no reserve that we accept all these sources of knowledge of God—nature, providence, Christian experience—as true and valid sources, the well-authenticated data yielded by which are to be received by us as revelations of God, and as such to be placed alongside of the revelations in the written Word and wrought with them into one system. As a matter of fact, theologians have always so dealt with them; and doubtless they always will so deal with them.

But to perceive, as all must perceive, that every method by which God manifests Himself, is, so far as this manifestation can be clearly interpreted, a source of knowledge of Him, and must, therefore, be taken account of in framing all our knowledge of Him into one organic whole, is far from allowing that there are no differences among these various manifestations—in the amount of revelation they give, the clearness of their message, the ease and certainty with which they may be interpreted, or the importance of the special truths which they are fitted to convey. Far rather is it *a priori* likely that if there are "divers manners" in which God has revealed Himself, He has not revealed precisely the same message through each; that these "divers manners" correspond also to divers messages of divers degrees of importance, delivered with divers degrees of clearness. And the mere fact that He has included in these "divers manners" a copious revelation in a written Word, delivered with an authenticating accompaniment of signs and miracles, proved by recorded prophecies with their recorded fulfillments, and pressed, with the greatest solemnity, upon the attention and consciences of men as the very Word of the Living God, who has by it made all the wisdom of men foolishness; nay, proclaimed as containing within itself the formulation of His truth, the proclamation of His law, the discovery of His plan of salvation: this mere fact, I say, would itself and prior to all comparison, raise an overwhelming presumption that all the others of "the divers manners" of God's revelation were insufficient for the purposes for which revelation is given, whether on account of defect in the amount of their communication or insufficiency of attestation or uncertainty of interpretation or fatal onesidedness in the character of the revelation they are adapted to give.

We need not be surprised, therefore, that on actual examination, such imperfections are found undeniably to attach to all forms of what we may, for the sake of discrimination, speak of as mere manifestations of God; and that thus the revelation of God in His written Word—in which are included the only authentic records of the revelation of Him through the incarnate Word—is easily shown not only to be incomparably superior to all other manifestations of Him in the fullness, richness, and clearness of its communications, but also to contain the sole discovery of much that it is most important for the soul to know as to its state and destiny, and of much that is most precious in our whole body of theological knowledge. The superior lucidity of this revelation makes it the norm of interpretation for what is revealed so much more darkly through the other methods of manifestation. The glorious character of the discoveries made in it throws all other manifestations into comparative shadow. The amazing fullness of its disclosures renders what they can tell us of little relative value. And its absolute completeness for the needs of man, taking up and reiteratingly repeating in the clearest of language all that can be wrung from their sometimes enigmatic indications, and then adding to this a vast body of still more momentous truth undiscoverable through them, all but supersedes their necessity. With the fullest recognition of the validity of all the knowledge of God and His ways with men, which can be obtained through the manifestations of His power and divinity in nature and history and grace; and the frankest allowance that the written Word is given, not to destroy the manifestations of God, but to fulfill them; the theologian must yet refuse to give these sources of knowledge a place alongside of the written Word, in any other sense than that he gladly admits that they, alike with it, but in unspeakably lower measure, do tell us of God. And nothing can be a clearer indication of a decadent theology or of a decaying faith, than a tendency to neglect the Word in favor of some one or of all of the lesser sources of theological truth, as fountains from which to draw our knowledge of divine things. This were to prefer the flickering rays of a taper to the blazing light of the sun; to elect to draw our water from a muddy run rather than to dip it from the broad bosom of the pure fountain itself.

Nevertheless, men have often sought to still the cravings of their souls with a purely natural theology; and there are men today who prefer to derive their knowledge of what God is and what He will do for man from an analysis of the implications of their own religious feelings: not staying to consider that nature, "red in tooth and claw with ravin," can but direct our eyes to the God of law, whose deadly letter kills; or that our feelings must needs point us to the God of our imperfect apprehension or of our unsanctified desires—not to the God that is, so much as to the God that we would fain should be. The natural result of resting on the revelations of nature is despair; while the inevitable end of making our appeal to even the Christian heart is to make for ourselves refuges of lies in which there is neither truth nor safety. We may, indeed, admit that it is valid reasoning to infer from the nature of the Christian life what are the modes of God's activities towards His children: to see, for instance, in conviction of sin and the sudden peace of the newborn soul, God's hand in slaying that He may make alive, His almighty power in raising the spiritually dead. But how easy to overstep the limits of valid inference; and, forgetting that it is the body of Christian truth known and assimilated that determines the type of Christian experience, confuse in our inferences what is from man with what is from God, and condition and limit our theology by the undeveloped Christian thought of the man or his times. The interpretation of the data included in what we have learned to call "the Christian conscious-ness," whether of the individual or of the church at large, is a process so delicate, so liable to error, so inevitably swayed to this side or that by the currents that flow up and down in the soul, that probably few satisfactory inferences could be drawn from it, had we not the norm of Christian experiences and its dogmatic implications recorded for us in the perspicuous pages of the written Word. But even were we to suppose that the interpretation was easy and secure, and that we had before us, in an infallible formula-tion, all the implications of the religious experience of all the men who have ever known Christ, we have no reason to believe that the whole body of facts thus obtained would suffice to give us a complete theology. After all, we know in part and we feel in part; it is only when that which is perfect shall appear that we shall know or experience all that Christ has in store for us. With the fullest acceptance, therefore, of the data of the theology of the feelings, no less than of natural theology, when their results are validly obtained and sufficiently authenticated as trustworthy, as divinely revealed facts which must be wrought into our system, it remains nevertheless true that we should be con-fined to a meager and doubtful theology were these data not confirmed, reinforced, and supplemented by the surer and fuller revelations of Scripture; and that the Holy Scriptures are the source of theology in not only a degree, but also a sense in which nothing else is.

There may be a theology without the Scriptures—a theology of nature, gathered by painful, and slow, and sometimes doubtful processes from what man sees around him in external nature and the course of history, and what he sees within him of nature and of grace. In like manner there may be and has been an astronomy of nature, gathered by man in his natural state without help from aught but his naked eyes, as he watched in the fields by night. But what is this astronomy of nature to the as-tronomy that has become possible through the wonderful appliances of our observatories? The Word of God is to theology as, but vastly more than, these instruments are to astronomy. It is the instrument which so far increases the possibilities of the science as to revolutionize it and to place it upon a height from which it can never more descend. What would be thought of the deluded man, who, discarding the new methods of research, should insist on acquiring all the astronomy which he would admit, from the unaided observation of his own myopic and astigmatic eyes? Much more deluded is he who, neglecting the instrument of God's Word written, would confine his admissions of theological truth to what he could discover from the broken lights that play upon external nature, and the faint gleams of a dying or even a slowly reviving light, which arise in his own sinful soul. Ah, no! The telescope first made a real science of astronomy possible: and the Scriptures form the only sufficing source of theology.

5. Under such a conception of its nature and sources, we are led to consider the place of systematic theology among the other theological disciplines as well as among the other sciences in general. Without encroaching upon the details of theological encyclopedia, we may adopt here the usual fourfold distribution of the theological disciplines into the exegetical, the historical, the systematic, and the practical, with only the correction of prefixing to them a fifth department of apologetical theology. The place of systematic theology in this distribution is determined by its relation to the preceding disciplines, of which it is the crown and head. Apologetical theology prepares the way for all theology by establishing its necessary presuppositions without which no theology is possible—the existence and essential nature of God, the religious nature of man which enables him to receive a revelation from God, the possibility of a revelation and its actual realization in the Scriptures. It thus places the Scriptures in our hands for investigation and study. Exegetical theology receives these inspired writings from the hands of apologetics, and inves-

tigates their meaning; presenting us with a body of detailed and substantiated results, culminating in a series of organized systems of biblical history, biblical ethics, biblical theology, and the like, which provide material for further use in the more advanced disciplines. Historical theology investigates the progressive realization of Christianity in the lives, hearts, worship, and thought of men, issuing not only in a full account of the history of Christianity, but also in a body of facts which come into use in the more advanced disciplines, especially in the way of the manifold experiments that have been made during the ages in Christian organization, worship, living, and creed-building, as well as of the sifted results of the reasoned thinking and deep experience of Christian truth during the whole past. Systematic theology does not fail to strike its roots deeply into this matter furnished by historical theology; it knows how to profit by the experience of all past generations in their efforts to understand and define, to systematize and defend revealed truth; and it thinks of nothing so little as lightly to discard the conquests of so many hard-fought fields. It therefore gladly utilizes all the material that historical theology brings it, accounting it, indeed, the very precipitate of the Christian consciousness of the past; but it does not use it crudely, or at first hand for itself, but accepts it as investigated, explained, and made available by the sister disciplines of historical theology, which alone can understand it or draw from it its true lessons. It certainly does not find in it its chief or primary source, and its relation to historical theology is, in consequence, far less close than that in which it stands to exegetical theology, which is its true and especial handmaid. The independence of exegetical theology is seen in the fact that it does its work wholly without thought or anxiety as to the use that is to be made of its results; and that it furnishes a vastly larger body of data than can be utilized by any one discipline. It provides a body of historical, ethical, liturgic, ecclesiastical facts, as well as a body of theological facts. But so far as its theological facts are concerned, it provides them chiefly that they may be used by systematic theology as material out of which to build its system.

This is not to forget the claims of biblical theology. It is rather to emphasize its value, and to afford occasion for explaining its true place in the encyclopedia, and its true relations on the one side to exegetical theology, and on the other to systematics—a matter which appears to be even yet imperfectly understood in some quarters. Biblical theology is not a section of historical theology, although it must be studied in a historical spirit, and has a historical face; it is rather the ripest fruit of exegetics, and exegetics has not performed its full task until its scattered results in the way of theological data are gathered up into a full and articulated system of biblical theology. It is to be hoped that the time will come when no commentary will be considered complete until the capstone is placed upon its fabric by closing chapters gathering up into systematized exhibits, the unsystematized results of the continuous exegesis of the text, in the spheres of history, ethics, theology, and the like. The task of biblical theology, in a word, is the task of coördinating the scattered results of continuous exegesis into a concatenated whole, whether with reference to a single book of Scripture or to a body of related books or to the whole scriptural fabric. Its chief object is not to find differences of conception between the various writers, though some recent students of the subject seem to think this is so much their duty, that when they cannot find differences they make them. It is to reproduce the theological thought of each writer or group of writers in the form in which it lay in their own minds, so that we may be enabled to look at all their theological statements at their angle, and to understand all their deliverances as modified and conditioned by their own point of view. Its exegetical value lies just in this circumstance, that it is only when we have thus concatenated an author's theological statements into a whole, that we can be sure that we understand them as he understood them in detail. A light is inevitably thrown back from biblical theology upon the separate theological deliverances as they occur in the text, such as subtly colors them, and often, for the first time, gives them to us in their true setting, and thus enables us to guard against perverting them when we adapt them to our use. This is a noble function, and could students of biblical theology only firmly grasp it, once for all, as their task, it would prevent this important science from being brought into contempt through a tendency to exaggerate differences in form of statement into divergences of view, and so to force the deliverances of each book into a strange and unnatural combination, in the effort to vindicate a function for this discipline.

The relation of biblical theology to systematic theology is based on a true view of its function. Systematic theology is not founded on the direct and primary results of the exegetical process; it is founded on the final and complete results of exegesis as exhibited in biblical theology. Not exegesis itself, then, but biblical theology, provides the material for systematics. Biblical theology is not, then, a rival of systematics; it is not even a parallel product of the same body of facts, provided by exegesis; it is the basis and source of systematics. Systematic theology is not a concatenated data given to it by biblical theology. It uses the individual data furnished by exegesis, in a word, not crudely, not independently for itself, but only after these data have been worked up into biblical theology and have received from it their final coloring and subtlest shades of meaning—in other words, only in their true sense, and after exegetics has said its last word upon them. Just as we shall attain our finest and truest conception of the person and work of Christ, not by crudely trying to combine the scattered details of His life and teaching as given in our four Gospels into one patchwork life and account of His teaching; but far more rationally and far more successfully by first catching Matthew's full conception of Jesus, and then Mark's, and then Luke's, and then John's, and combining these four conceptions into one rounded whole: so we gain our truest systematics not by at once working together the separate dogmatic statements in the Scriptures, but by combining them in their due order and proportion as they stand in the various theologies of the Scriptures. Thus we are enabled to view the future whole not only in its parts, but in the several combinations of the parts; and, looking at it from every side, to obtain a true conception of its solidity and strength, and to avoid all exaggeration or falsification of the details in giving them place in the completed structure. And thus we do not make our theology, according to our own pattern, as a mosaic, out of the fragments of the biblical teaching; but rather look out from ourselves upon it as a great prospect, framed out of the mountains and plains of the theologies of the Scriptures, and strive to attain a point of view from which we can bring the whole landscape into our field of sight.

From this point of view, we find no difficulty in understanding the relation in which the several disciplines stand to one another, with respect to their contents. The material that systematics draws from other than biblical sources may be here left momentarily out of account. The actual contents of the theological results of the exegetic process, of biblical theology, and of systematics, with this limitation, may be said to be the same. The immediate work of exegesis may be compared to the work of a recruiting officer: it draws out from the mass of mankind the men who are to constitute the army. Biblical theology organizes these men into companies and regiments and corps, arranged in marching order and accoutered for service. Systematic theology combines these companies and regiments and corps into an army—a single and unitary whole, determined by its own all-pervasive principle. It, too, is composed of men—the same men which were recruited by exegetics; but it is composed of these men, not as individuals merely, but in their due relations to the other men of their companies and regiments and corps. The simile is far from a perfect one; but it may illustrate the mutual rela-

tions of the disciplines, and also, perhaps, suggest the historical element that attaches to biblical theology, and the
element of all-inclusive systematization which is insepara-
ble from systematic theology. It is just this element, determining the spirit and therefore the methods of systematic
theology, which, along with its greater inclusiveness, dis-
criminates it from all forms of biblical theology, the spirit
of which is purely historical.

6. The place that theology, as the scientific presentation
of all the facts that are known concerning God and His
relations, claims for itself within the circle of the sciences is
an equally high one with that which it claims among the
theological disciplines. Whether we consider the topics
which it treats, in their dignity, their excellence, their
grandeur; or the certainty with which its data can be determined; or the completeness with which its principles
have been ascertained and its details classified; or the use-
fulness and importance of its discoveries: it is as far out of
all comparison above all other sciences as the eternal
health and destiny of the soul are of more value than this
fleeting life in this world. It is not so above them, however,
as not to be also a constituent member of the closely inter-
related and mutually interacting organism of the sciences.
There is no one of them all which is not, in some measure,
touched and affected by it, or which is not in some measure included in it. As all nature, whether mental or material, may be conceived of as only the mode in which God
manifests Himself, every science which investigates nature
and ascertains its laws is occupied with the discovery of the
modes of the divine action, and as such might be considered a branch of theology. And, on the other hand, as all
nature, whether mental or material, owes its existence to
God, every science which investigates nature and ascertains its laws, depends for its foundation upon that science
which would make known what God is and what the relations are in which He stands to the work of His hands and
in which they stand to Him; and must borrow from it those

conceptions through which alone the material with which it deals can find its explanation or receive its proper significance.

Theology, thus, enters into the structure of every other science. Its closest relations are, no doubt, with the highest of the other sciences, ethics. Any discussion of our duty to God must rest on a knowledge of our relation to Him; and much of our duty to man is undiscoverable, save through knowledge of our common relation to the one God and Father of all, and one Lord the Redeemer of all, and one Spirit the Sanctifier of all—all of which it is the function of theology to supply. This fact is, of course, not fatal to the existence of a natural ethics; but an ethics independent of theological conceptions would be a meager thing indeed, while the theology of the scriptural revelation for the first time affords a basis for ethical investigation at once broad enough and sure enough to raise that science to its true dignity. Accordingly, a purely natural ethics has always been an incomplete ethics even relatively to the less developed forms of ethics resting on a revealed basis. A careful student has recently told us, for example, that:

> Between the ethics of pagan antiquity and that of the Old Testament there is a difference of the widest and most radical kind. There is no trace of gradual transition from the one to the other. That difference is first seen in the pagan conception of God and of man's ethical relation to Him.... It was essentially a morality between man and man. For where man's relation to a personal God is not apprehended, anything approaching an universal ethics is impossible, and only individual virtues can be manifested. Ethics was thus deprived of its unity.... Morality became but a catalogue of separate virtues, and was deprived of that penetrating bond of union which it receives when the realm of human personalities is bound by innumerable links to the great central personality, God.[3]

We must not, however, on the ground of this intimacy of relation, confound the two sciences of theology and ethics. Something like it in kind and approaching it in degree exists between theology and every other science, no one of which is so independent of it as not to touch and be touched by it. Something of theology is implicated in all metaphysics and physics alike. It alone can determine the origin of either matter or mind, or of the mystic powers that have been granted to them.[4] It alone can explain the nature of second causes and set the boundaries to their efficiency. It alone is competent to declare the meaning of the ineradicable persuasion of the human mind that its reason is right reason, its processes trustworthy, its intuitions true. All science without God is mutilated science, and no account of a single branch of knowledge can ever be complete until it is pushed back to find its completion and ground in Him. In the eloquent words of Dr. Pusey:

> God alone *is* in Himself, and is the Cause and Upholder of everything to which He has given being. Every faculty of the mind is some reflection of His; every truth has its being from Him; every law of nature has the impress of His hand; everything beautiful has caught its light from His eternal beauty; every principle of goodness has its foundation in His attributes.... Without Him, in the region of thought, everything is dead; as without Him everything which is, would at once cease to be. All things must speak of God, refer to God, or they are atheistic. History, without God, is a chaos without design, or end, or aim. Political Economy, without God, would be a selfish teaching about the acquisition of wealth, making the larger portion of mankind animate machines for its production; Physics, without God, would be but a dull inquiry into certain meaningless phenomena; Ethics, without God, would be a varying rule, without principle, or substance, or centre, or regulating hand; Metaphysics, without God, would make man his own temporary god, to be resolved, after his brief hour here, into the nothingness out of which he proceeded.[5]

It is thus as true of sciences as it is of creatures, that in Him they all live and move and have their being. The science of Him and His relations is the necessary ground of all science. All speculation takes us back to Him; all inquiry presupposes Him; and every phase of science consciously or unconsciously rests at every step on the science that makes Him known. Theology, thus, as the science which treats of God, lies at the root of all sciences. It is true enough that each could exist without it, in a sense and in some degree; but through it alone can any one of them reach its true dignity. Herein we see not only the proof of its greatness, but also the assurance of its permanence. "What so permeates all sections and subjects of human thought, has a deep root in human nature and an immense hold upon it. What so possesses man's mind that he cannot think at all without thinking of it, is so bound up with the very being of intelligence that ere it can perish, intellect must cease to be."[6]

It is only in theology, therefore, that the other sciences find their completion. Theology, formally speaking, is accordingly the apex of the pyramid of the sciences by which the structure is perfected. Its relation to the other sciences is, thus, in this broader sphere quite analogous to its relation to the other branches of the theological encyclopedia in that narrower sphere. All other sciences are subsidiary to it, and it builds its fabric out of material supplied by them. Theology is the science which deals with the facts concerning God and His relations with the universe. Such facts include all the facts of nature and history: and it is the very function of the several sciences to supply these facts in scientific, that is, thoroughly comprehended form. Scientific theology thus stands at the head of the sciences as well as at the head of the theological disciplines. The several sciences deal each with its own material in an independent spirit and supply a multitude of results not immediately useful to theology. But so far as their results stand related to questions with which theology deals, they exist only to serve her. Dr. Flint well says:

> The relevant data of natural theology are all the works of God in nature and providence, all the phenomena and laws of matter, mind, and history,—and these can only be thoroughly ascertained by the special sciences. The surest and most adequate knowledge of them is knowledge in the

form called scientific, and therefore in this form the theologian must seek to know them. The sciences which deal with nature, mind, and history hold the same position towards natural theology which the disciplines that treat of the composition, genuineness, authenticity, text, development, etc., of the Scriptures do towards Biblical theology. They inform us, as it were, what is the true text and literal interpretation of the book of creation. Their conclusions are the premises, or at least the data, of the scientific natural theologian. All reasonings of his which disregard these data are *ipso facto* condemned. A conflict between the results of these sciences and the findings of natural theology is inconceivable. It would be a conflict between the data and conclusions of natural theology, and so equivalent for natural theology to self-contradiction. . . . The religion of the Bible. . . is but one of a multitude of religions which have left traces of themselves in documents, monuments, rites, creeds, customs, institutions, individual lives, social changes, etc., and there is a theological discipline— comparative theology—which undertakes to disclose the spirit, delineate the character, trace the development, and exhibit the relations of all religions with the utmost attainable exactitude. Obviously the mass of data which this science has to collect, sift, and interpret is enormous. They can only be brought to light and set in their natural relationships by the labours of hosts of specialists of all kinds. . . . Christian dogmatics has to make use of the results of natural theology, Biblical theology, and comparative theology, and to raise them to a higher stage by a comprehensive synthesis which connects them with the person and work of Christ, as of Him in whom all spiritual truth is comprehended and all spiritual wants supplied.[7]

The essence of the matter is here admirably set forth, though as connected with some points of view which may require modification. It would seem to be a mistake, for example, to conceive of scientific theology as the immediate and direct synthesis of the three sources—natural theology, biblical theology and comparative theology—so that it would be considered the product in like degree or even in similar manner of the three. All three furnish data for the completed structure; but if what has been said in an earlier connection has any validity, natural and compara-

tive theology should stand in a somewhat different relation
to scientific theology from that which biblical theology
occupies—a relation not less organic indeed, but certainly
less direct. The true representation seems to be that scientific theology is related to the natural and historical sciences, not immediately and independently for itself, but
only indirectly, that is, through the mediation of the pre-
liminary theological discipline of apologetics. The work of
apologetics in its three branches of philosophical,
psychological, and historical, results not only in presenting
the Bible to the theological student, but also in presenting
to him God, religion, and Christianity. And in so doing, it
supplies him with the total material of natural and comparative theology as well as with the foundation on which
exegesis is to raise the structure of biblical theology. The
materials thus provided scientific theology utilizes, just as
it utilizes the results of exegesis through biblical theology,
and the results of the age-long life of men under Christianity through historical theology. Scientific theology
rests, therefore, most directly on the results of biblical
exegesis as provided in biblical theology; but avails itself
likewise of all the material furnished by all the preceding
disciplines, and, in the results of apologetics as found in
natural theology and comparative theology, of all the data
bearing on its problems supplied by all the sciences. But it
does not make its direct appeal crudely and independently
to these sciences, any more than to exegesis and Christian
history, but as it receives the one set of results from the
hands of exegetics and historics, so it receives the others
from the hand of apologetics.[8] Systematic theology is fun-
damentally one of the theological disciplines, and bears
immediate relation only to its sister disciplines; it is only
through them that it reaches further out and sets its roots
in more remote sources of information.

7. The interpretation of a written document, intended
to convey a plain message, is infinitely easier than the interpretation of the teaching embodied in facts themselves.
It is therefore that systematic treatises on the several sci-

ences are written. Theology has, therefore, an immense advantage over all other sciences, inasmuch as it is more an inductive study of facts conveyed in a written revelation, than an inductive study of facts as conveyed in life. It was, consequently, the first-born of the sciences. It was the first to reach relative completeness. And it is today in a state far nearer perfection than any other science. This is not, however, to deny that it is a progressive science. In exactly the same sense in which any other science is progressive, this is progressive. It is not meant that new revelations are to be expected of truth which has not been before within the reach of man. There is a vast difference between the progress of a science and increase in its material. All the facts of psychology, for instance, have been in existence so long as mind itself has existed; and the progress of this science has been dependent on the progressive discovery, understanding, and systematization of these facts. All the facts of theology have, in like manner, been within the reach of man for nearly two millenniums; and the progress of theology is dependent on men's progress in gathering, defining, mentally assimilating, and organizing these facts into a correlated system. So long as revelation was not completed, the progressive character of theology was secured by the progress in revelation itself. And since the close of the canon of Scripture, the intellectual realization and definition of the doctrines revealed in it, in relation to one another, have been, as a mere matter of fact, a slow but ever advancing process.

The affirmation that theology has been a progressive science is no more, then, than to assert that it is a science that has had a history—and a history which can be and should be genetically traced and presented. First, the objective side of Christian truth was developed: pressed on the one side by the crass monotheism of the Jews and on the other by the coarse polytheism of the heathen, and urged on by its own internal need of comprehending the sources of its life, Christian theology first searched the Scriptures that it might understand the nature and modes of existence of its God and the person of its divine Redeemer. Then, more and more conscious of itself, it more and more fully wrought out from those same Scriptures a guarded expression of the subjective side of its faith; until through throes and conflicts it has built up the system which we all inherit. Thus the body of Christian truth has come down to us in the form of an organic growth; and we can conceive of the completed structure as the ripened fruit of the ages, as truly as we can think of it as the perfected result of the exegetical discipline. As it has come into our possession by this historic process, there is no reason that we can assign why it should not continue to make for itself a history. We do not expect the history of theology to close in our own day. However nearly completed our realization of the body of truth may seem to us to be; however certain it is that the great outlines are already securely laid and most of the details soundly discovered and arranged; no one will assert that every detail is as yet perfected, and we are all living in that confidence so admirably expressed by old John Robinson, "that God hath more truth yet to break forth from His holy Word." Just because God gives us the truth in single thread which we must weave into the reticulated texture, all the threads are always within our reach, but the finished texture is ever and will ever continue to be before us until we dare affirm that there is no truth in the Word which we have not perfectly apprehended, and no relation of these truths as revealed which we have not perfectly understood, and no possibility in clearness of presentation which we have not attained.

The conditions of progress in theology are clearly discernible from its nature as a science. The progressive men in any science are the men who stand firmly on the basis of the already ascertained truth. The condition of progress in building the structures of those great cathedrals whose splendid piles glorify the history of art in the Middle Ages, was that each succeeding generation should build upon the foundations laid by its predecessor. If each architect had begun by destroying what had been accomplished by his forerunners, no cathedral would ever have been raised.[9] The railroad is pushed across the continent by the simple process of laying each rail at the end of the line already laid. The prerequisite of all progress is a clear discrimination which as frankly accepts the limitations set by the truth already discovered, as it rejects the false and bad. Construction is not destruction; neither is it the outcome of destruction. There are abuses no doubt to be reformed; errors to correct; falsehoods to cut away. But the history of progress in every science and no less in theology is a story of impulses given, corrected, and assimilated. And when they have been once corrected and assimilated, these truths are to remain accepted. It is then time for another impulse, and the condition of all further progress is to place ourselves in this well-marked line of growth. Astronomy, for example, has had such a history; and there are now some indisputable truths in astronomy, as, for instance, the rotundity of the earth and the central place of the sun in our system. I do not say that these truths are undisputed; probably nothing is more undisputed in astronomy, or any other science, than in theology. At all events he who wishes, may read the elaborate arguments of the "Zetetic" philosophers, as they love to call themselves, who in this year of grace are striving to prove that the earth is flat and occupies the center of our system. Quite in the same spirit, there are "Zetetic" theologians who strive with similar zeal and acuteness to overturn the established basal truths of theology—which, however, can nevermore be shaken; and we should give about as much ear to them in the one science as in the other. It is utter folly to suppose that progress can be made otherwise than by placing ourselves in the line of progress; and if the temple of God's truth is ever to be completely built, we must not spend our efforts in digging at the foundations which have been securely laid in the distant past, but must rather give our best efforts to rounding the arches, carving the capitals, and fitting in the fretted roof. What if it is not ours to lay foundations? Let us rejoice that that work has been done! Happy are we if our God will permit us to bring a single capstone into place. This fabric is not a house of cards to be built and blown down again a hundred times a day, as the amusement of our idle hours: it is a miracle of art to which all ages and lands bring their varied tribute. The subtle Greek laid the foundations; the law-loving Roman raised high the walls; and all the perspicuity of France and ideality of Germany and systematization of Holland and deep sobriety of Britain have been expended in perfecting the structure; and so it grows.

We have heard much in these last days of the phrase "progressive orthodoxy," and in somewhat strange connections. Nevertheless, the phrase itself is not an inapt description of the building of this theological house. Let us assert that the history of theology has been and ever must be a progressive orthodoxy. But let us equally loudly assert that progressive orthodoxy and retrogressive heterodoxy can scarcely be convertible terms. Progressive orthodoxy implies that first of all we are orthodox, and secondly that we are progressively orthodox, that is, that we are ever growing more and more orthodox as more and more truth is being established. This has been and must be the history of the advance of every science, and not less among them, of the science of theology. Justin Martyr, champion of the orthodoxy of his day, held a theory of the intertrinitarian relationship which became heterodoxy after the Council of Nicea; the ever struggling Christologies of the earlier ages were forever set aside by the Chalcedon Fathers; Augustine determined for all time the doctrine of grace, Anselm the doctrine of the atonement, Luther the doctrine of forensic justification. In any progressive science, the amount of departure from accepted truth which is possible to the sound thinker becomes thus ever less and less, in proportion as investigation and study result in the progressive establishment of an ever increasing number of facts. The physician who would bring back today the medicine of Galen would be no more mad than the theologian who would revive the theology of Clement of Alexandria. Both were men of light and leading in their time; but their time is past, and it is the privilege of the child of today to know a sounder physic and a sounder theology than the giants of that far past yesterday could attain. It is of the very essence of our position at the end of the ages that we are ever more and more hedged around with ascertained facts, the discovery and establishment of which constitute the very essence of progress. Progress brings increasing limitation, just because it brings increasing knowledge. And as the orthodox man is he that teaches no other doctrine than that which has been established as true, the progressively orthodox man is he who is quick to perceive, admit, and condition all his reasoning by all the truth down to the latest, which has been established as true.

8. When we speak of progress our eyes are set upon a goal. And in calling theology a progressive science we unavoidably raise the inquiry, what the end and purpose is towards an ever increasing fitness to secure which it is continually growing. Its own completeness and perfecting as a science—as a department of knowledge—is naturally the proximate goal toward which every science tends. And when we consider the surpassing glory of the subject matter with which theology deals, it would appear that if ever science existed for its own sake, this might surely be true of this science. The truths concerning God and His relations are, above all comparison, in themselves the most worthy of all truths of study and examination. Yet we must vindicate a further goal for the advance of theology and thus contend for it that it is an eminently practical science. The contemplation and exhibition of Christianity as truth, is far from the end of the matter. This truth is specially communicated by God for a purpose, for which it is admirably adapted. That purpose is to save and sanctify the soul. And the discovery, study, and systematization of the truth is in order that, firmly grasping it and thoroughly comprehending it in all its reciprocal relations, we may be able to make the most efficient use of it for its holy pur-

pose. Well worth our most laborious study, then, as it is, for its own sake as mere truth, it becomes not only absorbingly interesting, but inexpressibly precious to us when we bear in mind that the truth with which we thus deal constitutes, as a whole, the engrafted Word that is able to save our souls. The task of thoroughly exploring the pages of revelation, soundly gathering from them their treasures of theological teaching, and carefully fitting these into their due places in a system whereby they may be preserved from misunderstanding, perversion, and misuse, and given a new power to convince the understanding, move the heart, and quicken the will, becomes thus a holy duty to our own and our brothers' souls as well as an eager pleasure of our intellectual nature.

That the knowledge of the truth is an essential prerequisite to the production of those graces and the building up of those elements of a sanctified character for the production of which each truth is especially adapted, probably few will deny: but surely it is equally true that the clearer, fuller, and more discriminating this knowledge is, the more certainly and richly will it produce its appropriate effect; and in this is found a most complete vindication of the duty of systematizing the separate elements of truth into a single soundly concatenated whole, by which the essential nature of each is made as clear as it can be made to human apprehension. It is not a matter of indifference, then, how we apprehend and systematize this truth. On the contrary, if we misconceive it in its parts or in its relations, not only do our views of truth become confused and erroneous, but also our religious life becomes dwarfed or contorted. The character of our religion is, in a word, determined by the character of our theology: and thus the task of the systematic theologian is to see that the relations in which the separate truths actually stand are rightly conceived, in order that they may exert their rightful influence on the development of the religious life. As no truth is so insignificant as to have no place in the development of our religious life, so no truth is so unimportant that we dare neglect it or deal deceitfully with it in adjusting it into our system. We are smitten with a deadly fear on the one side, lest by fitting them into a system of our own devising, we cut from them just the angles by which they were intended to lay hold of the hearts of men: but on the other side, we are filled with a holy confidence that, by allowing them to frame themselves into their own system as indicated by their own natures—as the stones in Solomon's temple were cut each for its place—we shall make each available for all men, for just the place in the saving process for which it was divinely framed and divinely given.

These theoretical considerations are greatly strengthened by the historical fact, that throughout all the ages every advance in the scientific statement of theological truth has been made in response to a practical demand, and has been made in a distinctly practical interest. We wholly misconceive the facts if we imagine that the development of systematic theology has been the work of cold, scholastic recluses, intent only upon intellectual subtleties. It has been the work of the best heart of the whole church driving on and utilizing in its practical interests, the best brain. The true state of the case could not be better expressed than it is by Professor Auguste Sabatier, when he tells us that:

> The promulgation of each dogma has been imposed on the Church by some practical necessity. It has always been to bring to an end some theological controversy which was in danger of provoking schism, to respond to attacks or accusations which it would have been dangerous to permit to acquire credit, that the Church has moved in a dogmatic way. . . . Nothing is more mistaken than to represent the Fathers of the Councils, or the members of the Synods as theoricians, or even as professional theologians, brought together in conference by speculative zeal alone, in order to resolve metaphysical enigmas. They were men of action, not of speculation; courageous priests and pastors who understood their mission, like soldiers in open battle, and whose first care was to save their Church, its life, its unity, its honor—ready to die for it as one dies for his country.[10]

In quite similar manner one of the latest critics (M. Pannier) of Calvin's doctrinal work feels moved to bear his testimony to the practical purpose which ruled over the development of his system. He says:

> In the midst, as at the outset of his work, it was the practical preoccupations of living faith which guided him, and never a vain desire for pure speculation. If this practical need led [in the successive editions of the "Institutes"] to some new theories, to many fuller expositions of principles, this was not only because he now desired his book to help students of theology to interpret Scripture better—it was because, with his systematic genius, Calvin understood all that which, from the point of view of their application, ideas gain severally in force by forming a complete whole around one master thought.[11]

Wrought out thus in response to practical needs, the ever growing body of scientific theology has worked its way among men chiefly by virtue of its ever increasing power of meeting their spiritual requirements. The story of the victory of Augustinianism in Southern Gaul, as brought out by Professor Arnold of Breslau, is only a typical instance of what each age has experienced in its own way, and with its own theological advances. He warns us that the victory of Augustinianism is not to be accounted for by the learning or dialectic gifts of Augustine, nor by the vigorous propaganda kept up in Gaul by the African refugees, nor by the influence of Caesarius, deservedly great as that was, nor by the pressure brought to bear from Rome: but rather by the fullness of its provision for the needs of the soul.

> These were better met by Christianity than by heathenism; by Catholicism than by Arianism; by the enthusiasm of asceticism than by the lukewarm worldliness of the old opponents of monachism; and they found more strength and consolation in the fundamental Augustinian conception of divine grace, than in the paltry mechanism of the synergistic moralism.[12]

Here is the philosophy, *sub specie temporis,* of the advance of doctrinal development; and it all turns on the progressively growing fitness of the system of doctrine to produce its practical fruits.[13]

It may possibly be thought, however, that these lessons are ill-applied to systematic theology properly so called: that it may be allowed indeed that the separate truths of religion make themselves felt in the life of men, but scarcely that the systematic knowledge of them is of any value for the religious life. Surely, however, we may very easily fall into error here. We do not possess the separate truths of religion in the abstract: we possess them only in their relations, and we do not properly know any one of them—nor can it have its full effect on our life—except as we know it in its relations to other truths, that is, as systematized. What we do not know, in this sense, systematically, we rob of half its power on our conduct; unless, indeed, we are prepared to argue that a truth has effect on us in proportion as it is unknown, rather than in proportion as it is known. To which may be added that when we do not know a body of doctrine systematically, we are sure to misconceive the nature of more or fewer of its separate elements; and to fancy, in the words of Dr. Charles Hodge, "that that is true which a more systematic knowledge would show us to be false," so that "our religious belief and therefore our religious life would become deformed and misshapen." Let us once more, however, strengthen our theoretical opinion by testimony: and for this let us appeal to the witness of a recent French writer who supports his own judgment by that of several of the best informed students of current French Protestantism.[14] Amid much external activity of Christian work, M. Arnaud tells us, no one would dare say that the life lived with Christ in God is flourishing in equal measure: and his conclusion is that, "in order to be a strong and living Christian, it does not suffice to submit our heart and will to the gospel: we must submit also our mind and our reason." He adds:

The doctrines of Christianity have just as much right to be believed as its duties have to be practised, and it is not permissible to accept these and reject those. In neglecting to inquire with care into the Biblical verities, and to assimilate them by reflection, the Christian loses part of his virtue, the preacher part of his force; both build their house on the sand or begin at the top; they deprive themselves of the precious lights which can illuminate and strengthen their faith, and fortify them against the frivolous or learned unbelief as well as against the aberrations of false individualism, that are so diffused in our day.

In support of this judgment he quotes striking passages, among others from Messrs. F. Bonifas and Ch. Bois. The former says:

What strikes me today is the incomplete and fragmentary character of our faith: the lack of precision in our Christian conceptions; a certain ignorance of the wonderful things which God has done for us and which He has revealed to us for the salvation and nourishment of our souls. I discover the traces of this ignorance in our preaching as well as in our daily life. And here is one of the causes of the feebleness of spiritual life in the bosom of our flocks and among ourselves. To these fluid Christian convictions, there necessarily corresponds a lowered Christian life.[15]

Mr. Bois similarly says:

There does not at present exist among us a strongly concatenated body of doctrine, possessing the conscience and determining the will. We have convictions, no doubt, and even strong and active convictions, but they are, if I may so speak, isolated and merely juxtaposed in the mind, without any deep bond uniting them into an organism.... Upon several fundamental points, even among believers, there is a vagueness, an indetermination, which leaves access open to every fluctuation and to the most unexpected mixtures of belief. Contradictory elements often live together and struggle with one another, even in the most positively convinced, without their suspecting the enmity of the guests they have received into their thought. It is astonishing to observe the strange amalgams which spring up and acclimate themselves in the minds of the young theological generations, which have been long deprived of the strong discipline of the past. This incoherence of ideas produces weakness and danger elsewhere also, besides in the sphere of doctrine. It is impossible but that spiritual life and practical activity should sustain also serious damage from this intellectual anarchy.[16]

Cannot we see in the state of French Protestantism as depicted in these extracts, a warning to ourselves, among whom we may observe the beginnings of the same doctrinal anarchy? And shall we not, at least, learn this much: that doctrine is in order to life, and that the study of doctrine must be prosecuted in a spirit which would see its end in the correction and edification of life? Shall we not, as students of doctrine, listen devoutly to the words of one of the richest writers on experimental religion of our generation, when he tells us that

> Living knowledge of our living Lord, and of our need of Him, and of our relations to Him for peace, life, testimony, service, consistency, is given by the Holy Comforter alone. But it is given by Him in the great rule of His dealings with man, only through the channel of doctrine, of revealed, recorded, authenticated truth concerning the Lord of life.

And shall we not catch the meaning of the illustrations which he adds:

> Does the happy soul, happy because brought to the "confidence of self-despair," and to a sight of the foundation of all peace, find itself saying, "O Lamb of God, I come," and know that it falls, never to be cast out, into the embraces of ever-living love? Every element in that profound experience of restful joy has to do with doctrine, applied by the Spirit. "O lamb of God" would be a meaningless incantation were it not for the precious and most definite doctrine of the sacrifice of propitiation and peace. That I *may* "come just as I am" is a matter of pure Divine information. My emotions, my deepest and most awful convictions, without such information, say the opposite; my instinct is to cry, "Depart, for I am a sinful man." The blessed doctrine, not my reveries, says, "Nay; He was wounded for thy trans-

gressions; come unto him.'... And when [one]... draws towards the journey's end, and exchanges the trials of the pilgrimage for the last trial, "the river that hath no bridge," why does he address himself in peace to die, this man who has been taught the evil of his own heart and the holiness of the Judge of all? It is because of doctrine. He knows the covenant of peace, and the Mediator of it. He knows, and he knows it through revealed doctrine only, that to depart is to be with Christ, and is far better. He knows that the sting of death is sin, and the strength of sin is the law. But he knows, with the same certainty, that God giveth us the victory through our Lord Jesus Christ; and that His sheep shall never perish; and that He will raise up again at the last day him that has come to God through Him. All this is doctrine. It is made to live in the man by the Holy Ghost given to him. But it is in itself creed, not life. It is revealed information.[17]

If such be the value and use of doctrine, the systematic theologian is preëminently a preacher of the gospel; and the end of his work is obviously not merely the logical arrangement of the truths which come under his hand, but the moving of men, through their power, to love God with all their hearts and their neighbors as themselves; to choose their portion with the Saviour of their souls; to find and hold Him precious; and to recognize and yield to the sweet influences of the Holy Spirit whom He has sent. With such truth as this he will not dare to deal in a cold and merely scientific spirit, but will justly and necessarily permit its preciousness and its practical destination to determine the spirit in which he handles it, and to awaken the reverential love with which alone he should investigate its reciprocal relations. For this he needs to be suffused at all times with a sense of the unspeakable worth of the revelation which lies before him as the source of his material, and with the personal bearings of its separate truths on his own heart and life; he needs to have had and to be having a full, rich, and deep religious experience of the great doctrines with which he deals; he needs to be living close to his God, to be resting always on the bosom of his Redeemer, to be filled at all times with the manifest influences of the Holy Spirit. The student of systematic theology needs a very sensitive religious nature, a most thoroughly consecrated heart, and an outpouring of the Holy Ghost upon him, such as will fill him with that spiritual discernment, without which all native intellect is in vain. He needs to be not merely a student, not merely a thinker, not merely a systematizer, not merely a teacher—he needs to be like the beloved disciple himself in the highest, truest, and holiest sense, a divine.

Reprinted with permission of Presbyterian and Reformed Publishing Co., from *Studies in Theology* by B. B. Warfield. Copyright 1932 by B. B. Warfield.

# Notes to Chapter 10

1. D. W. Simon, "The Nature and Scope of Systematic Theology," in *Bibliotheca Sacra*, li. (1894), p. 587.
2. Simon, "The Nature and Scope of Systematic Theology," p. 592.
3. W. S. Bruce, "The Ethics of the Old Testament" (1895), pp. 12–14.
4. Cf. the ground-texts which Professor Laidlaw has placed at the head of the first division of his "The Bible Doctrine of Man" (1895): "The truth concerning the soul can only be established by the word of God." —Plato, "Timaeus," 72 D. "How can the knowledge of the substance of the rational soul be sought or had from philosophy? It must surely be derived from the same divine inspiration from which the substance of the soul first emanated." —Bacon, "De Augmentis Scientiarum," lib. iv. cap. iii. 3.
5. E. B. Pusey, "Collegiate and Professorial Teaching and Discipline" (Oxford: Parker, 1854), pp. 215–16.
6. A. M. Fairbairn, "Theology As an Academic Discipline," in *Contemporary Review*, li. (1887), p. 202.
7. *Encyclopaedia Britannica*, 9th ed., s.v. "Theology."
8. It may be useful to seek to give a rough graphic representation of the relations of systematic theology as thus far outlined:

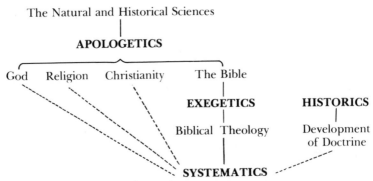

9, "Commend me," says Coleridge, "to the Irish architect who took out the foundation stone to repair the roof" (Anima Poetae," 1895), p. 139. Such architects seem to be rather numerous in the sphere of theology.

10. A. Sabatier, "Esquisse d'une philosophie de la religion," 1897, p. 306; cf. "The Vitality of Christian Dogmas" (London, 1898), pp. 31–33.

11. Jacques Pannier, "Le Témoignage du Saint-Esprit" (1893), p. 79.

12. C. F. Arnold, "Caesarius von Arelate" (1894), p. 343.

13. It is only another way of saying this to say with Professor W. M. Ramsay, when speaking of another of the great controversies (*Expositor,* January, 1896, [Fifth Series, iii.], p. 52): "Difficult, however, as it is to appreciate the real character of the Arian controversy as a question of social life, on the whole we gather, I think, that the progressive tendencies were on the side of Basil, and acquiescence in the existing standard of morality characterized the Arian point of view. The 'Orthodox' Church was still the champion of higher aspirations, and Basil, however harsh he was to all who differed from him, was an ennobling and upward-struggling force in the life of his time."

14. Arnaud, "Manuel de dogmatique" (1890), p. ix.

15. "De la valeur religieuse des doctrines chrétiennes," p. 14.

16. *Revue théologique* de Montauban, 13ᵉ Année, p. 14.

17. Principal H. C. G. Moule, in his paper entitled "On the Relations Between Doctrine and Life," printed in "The Church and Her Doctrine" (New York: Christian Literature Co., 1892), pp. 185–88.

*John Jefferson Davis*

# 11

# Contextualization and the Nature of Theology

The term "contextualization," increasingly prominent in recent theological discussions, has significant implications for the way evangelicals understand the nature and task of systematic theology. In this chapter I will attempt to delineate some of the antecedents of the concept, draw contrasts with traditional conservative conceptions of the nature of theology, anticipate some possible objections to the newer view, and suggest some applications for theological education.

## Antecedents of Contextualization

The term "contextualization" appears to have first been used in a document prepared by the directors of the Theological Education Fund with reference to theological education in the Third World:

> [Contextualization] means all that is implied in the familiar term "indigenization" and yet seeks to press beyond. Contextualization has to do with how we assess the peculiarity of third-world contexts. Indigenization tends to be used in the sense of responding to the gospel in terms of a traditional culture. Contextualization, while not ignoring this, takes into account the process of secularity, technology, and the struggle for human justice, which characterizes the historical moment of nations in the Third World.[1]

While bearing considerable similarity to the older concept of "indigenization," contextualization, in the view of these writers, carries historical and political overtones not so prominent in the earlier terminology. The link with indigenization does, however, clearly point to the missiological context of many of the recent discussions of contextualization. Missiologists, missionary anthropologists, and Bible translators, long concerned with the development of "indigenous theologies" and indigenous churches, are at the present time some of the leading proponents of an understanding of theology which is context-specific and informed by cross-cultural awareness.[2] Third World reactions to the history of colonialism, the rising tides of national self-consciousness, and the challenges of Bible translation have all challenged missiologists to become increasingly sophisticated in attempting to distinguish transcultural biblical content from the Euro-American form in which it has historically been communicated. Resources from the newer disciplines of cross-cultural anthropology, communications theory, and linguistics are being used in order to develop biblical theologies which are dynamically equivalent for the specific cultural setting in which the missionary or Bible translator is working. The implication seems clear that systematic theology must also incorporate the insights of these newer disciplines in its own methodology, while retaining its classical relationship to exegesis, the history of doctrine, and philosophy.

Missiological discussions, while forming the most immediate horizon of the concern for contextualization, are hardly its sole antecedents. Other streams of influence contributing to this current would include the rise of the historical-critical method in biblical scholarship; the Marxist tradition and the discipline known as the sociology of knowledge; the hermeneutical concerns of existential theologians such as Bultmann and Tillich; the political theologies of the 1960s; and more recently, liberation theology in its Latin American, Black, feminist, American Indian, and Asian varieties.

A basic prerequisite for recognizing the need for contextualization in contemporary theology is a recognition of the context-specific nature of biblical revelation itself.[3] Contextualization is not a recent discovery of missiologist and liberation theologians, but is already a reality within the canon itself. The rise of the historical-critical method of the study of Scripture, while largely destructive in its initial stages, has forced traditional confessional theologies to recognize the real diversity within the canon, and has provided a necessary check against the tendency to press, in the interests of systematization, harmonization beyond its proper limits. The historical-critical method, in insisting that the biblical text be understood in the integrity of its own peculiar historical and cultural horizon of meaning, could really be understood as a recognition of "contextualization at the starting point of the hermeneutical trajectory." In contrast, systematic theology is concerned with the contemporary terminus of that same trajectory.

It cannot be said that evangelical theology as a whole has fully come to terms with the methodological implications of the historical-critical method. The ongoing discussions concerning the authority of Scripture reflect the tensions which still exist in this area. Nevertheless, it must be recognized that the rise of historical thinking in the eighteenth and especially in the nineteenth century constitutes a fundamental development in modern intellectual history which is unlikely to be reversed.[4] The greater awareness of the diversity within the biblical documents and their contextual rootedness brought about by the historical-critical method is a result which is here to stay. While the historical-critical method is not the enemy of theological coherence per se, it does challenge traditional understandings of theological systematization and even traditional understandings of the correspondence and coherence theories of truth. This latter point will be further developed in the closing section of the chapter.[5]

The theme of contextualization also has clear intellectual affinities with the discipline which has come to be known as the sociology of knowledge. Pioneers in this field such as Emile Durkheim, Karl Mannheim, Max Weber, and Max Scheler in their various ways emphasized the influence of the social environment on the form and content of human thought. This recognition of a strong sociological component in the shaping of human consciousness reflects the influence of the Marxist tradition.[6] It is unnecessary, of course, to adopt either a materialistic or deterministic view of history in order to appreciate the elements of truth in this perspective. The calls for the contextualization of the gospel (in actuality, a *re*contextualization) are simply based on the recognition of the need to communicate the faith in a context-specific fashion, and to make a critical assessment of the ways in which the church's or theologian's own social situation may be distorting the understanding of the message. The call for contextualization can become the occasion for gaining a heightened awareness of the danger of an enculturated gospel, a form of the Christian faith too closely amalgamated with the dominant values of the culture. Contextualization, like the sociology of knowledge, can then function as a self-critical tool for systematic theology.[7]

Contemporary discussions of contextualization also recall some of the basic themes of the "political theology" of the 1960s, as espoused by such writers as Cox, Metz, and Moltmann, and the more recent theologies of liberation in their various forms. During the 1960s many contemporary theologians were insisting that politics and social change constituted the basic hermeneutical horizon for theology. Not abstract speculations about an other-worldly life to come, but concrete actions to promote human freedom in the present, it was said, are theology's primary concern. Authentic theological reflection takes place only within the concrete context of political praxis.[8]

The political theologies of the 1960s were superseded by the liberation theologies of the 1970s. Common to the theologies of both decades was a concentration on the social and political context as the horizon of theological reflection. Latin American and Black theologians often criticized European theologians for what appeared to them to be relatively abstract and theoretical theologies of social change, but agreed with the earlier concern for doing theology in the light of the specific needs arising out of one's social context.[9] Again, one does not need to subscribe to a predominantly temporal and this-worldly understanding of salvation in order to appreciate the value of self-consciously reflecting on the sociopolitical contextualization of the gospel. Evangelicals can affirm with liberation theologians and recent proponents of the theme of contextualization the integral link between orthodoxy and orthopraxis in any given social context.

Even prior to the 1960s "existentialist" theologians such as Bultmann and Tillich were involved in their own form of contextualization. In this theological tradition, which might also be called "hermeneutical theology," the overriding question was, in the words of Tillich, "Can the Christian message be adapted to the modern mind without losing its essential and unique character?"[10] For both Bultmann and Tillich the existentialist philosophy of Martin Heidegger illuminated the situation of modern man and provided a hermeneutical link between biblical text and contemporary context. More recently, continuing in this existentialist vein, Helmut Thielicke has emphasized the nature of theology as being a contemporary "address" and "actualization" of the biblical word.[11] Evangelicals, while rightfully concerned about the very real dangers of an extra-biblical philosophy assuming a dominant position within the theological system, are increasingly recognizing the need to be both biblical and contemporary in their theologies, addressing the concerns of their own life-situations without dissolving the biblical substance.

## Conservative Theology and Contextualization

While all theologies have been addressed to their own situations, and thus implicitly "contextualized," it has not been until the modern period, especially with the rapid rise of the historical mode of thinking in the nineteenth century, that this fact has been self-consciously taken into account as a basic methodological issue for systematic theology. Protestant theology since the Enlightenment has increasingly come to recognize its own historicity and the historical limitations of its own cognitive horizons. For our purposes it will be useful to compare some older and newer understandings of the nature and task of systematic theology as found among representative conservative writers.

According to Charles Hodge, one of the prime architects of the Old Princeton theology, the basic task of systematic theology is ". . . the exhibition of the facts of Scripture in their proper order and relation, with the principles of general truths involved in the facts themselves, and which pervade and harmonize the whole."[12] For Hodge, who can be taken as a representative of the traditional conservative understanding of the nature of theology, the task of theology is to systematize the facts of the Bible, just as the task of the natural scientist is to systematize the facts of nature. While Hodge in practice did interact in his *Systematic Theology* with the theological and philosophical positions of his own contemporaries, the notion of theology as a word of contemporary "address" is not fundamental in Hodge's own understanding. By taking the natural sciences as something of a paradigm for theological method, the historicity of the theological enterprise is obscured. The result is a rather ahistorical understanding of the nature of theology, an understanding which certainly does not take into account the sociopolitical context of the theologian's own reflections.

The strength of Hodge's somewhat positivistic understanding of theological method is that it clearly assigns to the teaching of Scripture the role of an objective norm by which all theological assertions are to be tested. The weakness of this understanding is that it tends to obscure the role of *creative imagination* in the construction of the theological system. As David Kelsey and Michael Polanyi have shown, positivistic understandings of both theology and natural science have neglected the role of insight and creative intuition in the grasping of the peculiar gestalts arising in these disciplines.[13] Such a misunderstanding of the nature of theological reflection not only fails to accurately mirror the real nature of theologizing, but may also, as James Barr has suggested,[14] be one of the prime factors in the stifling of creativity among conservative theologians. The theologian's task is not merely to repeat past formulations of the "system," but to grasp afresh the "essence of Christianity" for his own situation and to express it in a manner appropriate to the given context. This, I take it, is an essential implication of the concept of contextualization for evangelical theology.

There are signs that evangelical theologians are beginning to see the importance of the concept of contextualization for the way they understand their own task. Stanley Gundry, in a presidential address to the Evangelical Theological Society, raised the following significant questions:

> I wonder if we really recognize that all theology represents a contextualization, even our own theology? We speak of Latin American liberation theology, black theology, or feminist theology; but without the slightest second thought we will assume that our own theology is simply theology, undoubtedly in its purest form. Do we recognize that the versions of evangelical theology held to by most people in this room are in fact North American, white, and male and that they reflect and/or address those values and concerns?[15]

It is encouraging to see such self-critical awareness in evangelical circles. We can believe that through divine revelation we have been made the recipients of absolute truths, and yet at the same time recognize the historicity and incompleteness of our own formulations. Such cognitive humility is helpful in relating to Christians of different theological persuasions.

Carl F. H. Henry, long a leader in American evangelical

circles, has restated the need for conservative thinkers to articulate fresh expressions of the faith:

> Evangelical theology is heretical if it is only creative and unworthy if it is only repetitious ... One often hears that non-evangelical theology seems to speak more directly to the dilemmas of the age but that its message forfeits the timeless biblical heritage. Evangelical theology, on the other hand, while preserving the Judeo-Christian verities all too often fail to project engagingly upon present-day perplexities.[16]

While not using the terminology of contextualization, Henry is calling for evangelicals to produce adequately contextualized biblical theologies for our own historical situation.

Clark Pinnock, in an inaugural lecture at McMaster Divinity College in Hamilton, Ontario, urged evangelicals to adopt a "bi-polar" method in both theology and preaching. "We should strive to be faithful to historic Christian beliefs taught in Scripture, and *at the same time* to be authentic and responsible to the contemporary hearers."[17] Pinnock, like Carl Henry and other evangelicals today, is in his own way calling for a newly contextualized evangelical theology.

### Contextualization: Unnecessary and Dangerous?

At this point it might be well to respond to a number of objections to the whole concept of contextualization which may have arisen in the mind of the reader. It might seem that contextualization is unnecessary, since evangelicals presumably are seeking only a "pure biblical theology"— and the content of Scripture is presumably the same from one context to another. Or, on the other hand, it might seem that the program of contextualization is inherently dangerous, in that it inevitably leads either to cognitive relativism or to some form of syncretism. Each of these possible objections is worthy of separate comment.

"Since evangelical theology is simply the theology of the

Bible, and since biblical truth is unchanging, discussions of 'contextualization' may be necessary in homiletics or counseling, but not in systematics." This objection goes straight to the heart of our understanding of the nature of theology itself. I would argue that there are a number of problems with this view of the nature of systematic theology. First of all, if systematic theology is essentially a "biblical theology" which merely repeats and arranges the statements and categories of Scripture, then which "biblical theology" is the really biblical one? The Lutheran? The Reformed? The Wesleyan? The dispensational? The very variety of theological systems within the evangelical tradition alone, all claiming an equally high regard for the authority of Scripture, is in itself an indication that there are factors beyond the text itself which shape the gestalt of the system. In no case does the exegete or theologian come to the text completely free of presuppositions. We can to a degree become more critically aware of our presuppositions, but we cannot eliminate them entirely. There is an inescapable element of personal judgment which shapes the theologian's vision, just as it does the artist's or scientist's.

There is a further difficulty in this objection in that it fails to clearly distinguish the tasks of biblical theology and systematic theology. At this point I find Krister Stendahl's formulation helpful: biblical theology is concerned with the historical and descriptive question of "what it meant"; systematic theology is concerned with the contemporary and normative question, "what it means."[18] The exegete or biblical theologian is concerned to recover the meaning of Isaiah's or Paul's or John's message in the full integrity of its original historical situation. The exegete, we might say, is concerned with "historical hermeneutics," while the systematician is concerned with "contemporary hermeneutics." The exegete *qua* exegete need not be concerned with how the Pauline doctrine of "principalities and powers" might be related to a Jungian theory of archetypes or to the structures of modern multinational corporations, but such questions inevitably face the systematician. The systematic theologian is faced with the fact that at many points our cosmological, scientific, and psychological categories differ from those of the writers of Scripture. Consequently, some type of "translation" of categories must occur during the process of theological reflection. The type of translation appropriate will vary with the historical situation and with the audience addressed. In any case, in both theology and preaching, it is not adequate to simply repeat the categories of Scripture. These categories must be taken up into the living consciousness of the interpreter and reexpressed in such a form as to produce a response in the contemporary receptor which is dynamically equivalent to the original response.

In this connection, a distinction between "doctrine" and "theology" is helpful. Doctrine can be defined as a straightforward summary of biblical teaching on any subject; theology is secondary reflection on the content of biblical doctrine.[19] The exegete attempts to recover the full historical meaning of Paul's understanding of justification by faith; the doctrine/historical theologian recovers what this meant for Luther; the systematic theologian, reflecting on these historically mediated meanings, may attempt to relate this to contemporary psychological categories of self-image, self-acceptance, and the like. Biblical doctrine is fixed in time, but systematic theology is not. In every age the theologian is challenged to reappropriate the scriptural content and to reflect it within the living consciousness of the believing community.

Another type of objection sees contextualization as inherently dangerous for the integrity of the content of theology. Does not such a program, it might be asked, inevitably lead either to a skeptical relativism, or to some form of syncretism of gospel and culture? In either case, the essential substance of the Christian message would be compromised.

The first objection might be restated as follows: If all acts of human understanding and self-expression are inextricably linked to the cultural categories of a specific historical milieu, then is it really possible to find a common basis for understanding between heterogeneous cultural contexts? In other words, if contextualization is carried out in a thoroughgoing manner, does this not in fact preclude adequate understanding by those standing outside the cultural milieu in which the message was originally encoded? Some Black theologians, for example, have claimed that whites are inherently incapable of understanding Black theology, since without having experienced real oppression, they lack the essential experiential preunderstanding which is the hermeneutical *a priori* of Black theology.[20] Similarly, it is suggested that males cannot fully understand feminist theology, or North Americans Latin American liberation theology, etc. Such claims, while having considerable degree of plausibility—especially during an era of heightened ethnic and cultural pluralism, scholarly discussions of cultural conditioning, and the like—nevertheless are susceptible to criticism on epistemological, anthropological, and theological grounds.

Epistemologically, the position in question, which can be called "perspectivism," assumes that the perception of meaning is totally dependent on the perspective of the observer. This position, a version of the Kantian view that human experience is constituted by the *a priori* categories of the human mind, is based on a metaphor of visual perception. A table, for example, presents different appearances to an observer, depending on whether the table is viewed from above, from the side, or from an angle. No two observers standing in different places, it is said, see exactly the same table. But does this in fact mean that the two observers cannot communicate with one another and agree on a commonly perceived table? Common sense and the ordinary experience of successful communication between human subjects indicate that this is not the case.[21] In spite of the physically different retinal images, each observer, through the tacit powers of the human mind, is able to achieve an imaginative integration of the visual particulars in a gestalt of meaning which transcends those particulars.[22] The human ability to transcend a given perspective is evident not only in the physiological sphere, but in the intellectual as well. Human beings, as bearers of the *Imago Dei*, are inherently self-transcending creatures. We are inevitably conditioned by our own historical perspectives, but we are not totally imprisoned by them.

Anthropologically, the relativistic thesis tends to overlook the basic commonalities of human nature which transcend racial, sexual, and ethnic lines. All human racial groups can in fact interbreed; all human languages are translatable to a degree which permits adequate cross-cultural communication; all human beings share basic bodily functions and needs; all human beings are subject to primal emotions such as fear, anxiety, happiness, loneliness, and jealousy; all cultures have ways of ritualizing basic life-passages such as birth, marriage, and death. In spite of great diversity in cultural *forms*, there appear to be a great many human activities which perform similar social *functions* in virtually all cultures.[23] There is remarkable commonality of basic human needs and social functions designed to fulfill those needs, whether we happen to be speaking of second-millennium Hebrew culture, or first-century Greco-Roman culture, or twentieth-century Euro-American culture. The commonality existing between diverse cultures is extensive enough to call into question what E. D. Hirsch has termed the historicist's "fallacy of the inscrutable past."[24] It may require a considerable expenditure of time and energy to understand a culture alien to our own, but the task is not impossible. This possibility is demonstrated over and over again by the daily labors of exegetes, archaeologists, historians, anthropologists, missionaries, and Bible translators.

Theologically, the thesis of perspectivism is called into question by certain fundamental unifying strands in the Christian faith. In spite of great diversity of formulation over the centuries, authentic expressions of Christian faith have always tended to show commonality in such fundamental doctrines as the doctrines of God and Christ. The

God of Christian faith is the one God who made heaven and earth, and who is the God and Father of Jesus Christ. The New Testament, in the midst of all its diversity, gives a common witness to the unity existing between the man Jesus of Nazareth and the resurrected, exalted Lord.[25] The great ecumenical creeds of the early church such as the Apostles' Creed and the formula of Chalcedon have been well-nigh universally received as authentic expositions of the Christian faith. While historical studies have demonstrated that the boundaries between orthodoxy and heresy were much more fluid, especially in the earliest centuries, than had been previously believed,[26] it is nonetheless quite possible for the believing community, on the basis of the tradition and the parameters indicated by the canonical documents themselves, to draw lines between creative contextualizations of the faith and heretical distortions of it. In the heat of doctrinal controversy, the task may be enormously difficult, but it is not in principle impossible, as the history of Christianity itself shows.

Finally, to conclude this section, a word is in order about the dangers of syncretism. It cannot be denied that there is an element of risk involved in all attempts to recontextualize the Christian message. The history of the Christian church has been the history of successive attempts to contextualize the gospel, some successful, some less so. From the time of the apostles, through the early apologists, medieval scholastics, Reformation and orthodox theologies, and the modern period, there has been a succession of efforts to communicate and defend the faith in relation to the issues and thought forms of the day. As we have already noted, it is not so much the *fact* of contextualization, but rather the methodological *self-consciousness* of that fact which is new. Conservatives, while quite sensitive to the syncretistic tendencies of the liberal experiment in theology, are often less aware of more subtle forms of syncretism which amalgamate the gospel with certain traditional cultural values. There can be a "heresy of tradition" as well as a "heresy of innovation."[27] Contextualization does entail the risk of syncretism, but that task must be undertaken if the gospel is to be faithfully preached and the Christian mission advanced.

## Implications for the Seminary

In conclusion, I would like to suggest, in rather brief fashion, a number of possible implications of this entire subject for the task of theological education. These suggestions are intended as points of departure for further reflection, rather than as finished conclusions.

1. It would seem that the notion of contextualization challenges teachers of theology to actively promote a spirit of *creativity* and *innovation* in students as they learn the content and methodology of systematic theology. There are many in conservative circles who are understandably suspicious of "creativity" in theology, suggesting as it does some of the more unfortunate vagaries and fads of modern theology. Nevertheless, an overemphasis on the conservative as opposed to the constructive task of theology can lead to stagnation and sterility in our theology. We must risk greater trust in the ability of the Holy Spirit to filter the content of biblical revelation through the life-experiences of our students and to produce fresh articulations of the faith. Our task is to challenge our students to both conserve the unchanging content of Scripture, and to creatively apply it to their own contemporary contexts of ministry.

2. The theme of contextualization is one which suggests a model for understanding the integration of the theological curriculum. Many of the tensions which so frequently exist between the theoretical and practical disciplines can be largely overcome when systematicians understand the contextual nature of their own discipline. If one defines systematic theology as, say, "systematic reflection on Scripture and the contemporary context of ministry in mutual relation, with Scripture as the norm," then an integral link

is forged between systematics and ministry. Such a practice-based conception of theology is neither purely pragmatic nor purely theoretical. Such a conception of the nature of theology could be quite helpful in relating programs of field education to classroom theological instruction.

Tension between the disciplines is sometimes most acutely felt at the interface of biblical studies and systematic theology. When it is realized that both the exegete and the systematician are concerned with contextualized theologies—at different ends of the hermeneutical trajectory—much of this tension is overcome. Both disciplines employ methods which are historically and contextually oriented.

The relationship between historical and systematic studies is, on this predicate, a natural one. The history of the church is largely the history of successive contextualizations of the Christian message. Systematic reflection is a continuation of this process.

The relationship between theology and missions and evangelism is also seen to be an integral one in this model. If theology is inherently task-oriented, and rightly functions only within the context of the ongoing mission of the church, then theology is seen as mission-oriented reflection, and missions are seen as inherently theological.[28] Such an understanding seems especially timely in view of the likelihood that issues arising in the areas of missiology, ecclesiology, and church and society will continue to be important foci of theological reflection during the decades ahead.

3. The concept of contextualization has implications for the way we understand the sources of theological and hermeneutical studies. Traditionally, discussions of the sources of theology have distinguished between Scripture as a primary source and philosophy, the history of doctrine, and church history as secondary sources. Today, the understanding of secondary sources in theology is being enlarged to include the social sciences, especially psychol-

ogy, sociology (including the sociology of knowledge), cross-cultural anthropology, and communications theory. No evangelical theologian can afford to ignore these disciplines today. Traditional concerns for philosophy and a "natural theology of God" are being supplemented, though not replaced, by new currents from the social sciences and the "hermeneutics of the phenomenon of man." In the areas of biblical and theological hermeneutics, the older and narrower concerns with philology, history, and philosophy will likewise be broadened by the new data of the social sciences. Historical-grammatical hermeneutics becomes *historical-cultural* hermeneutics in the newer conceptuality.

4. Contextualization has implications for the ongoing discussions concerning the nature of the authority of Scripture. Insofar as discussions of contextualization in contemporary theology lead us to a renewed appreciation of the contextual and task-oriented nature of the New Testament documents, then we may be in a position to see such questions as the nature of factual correspondence and accuracy vis-a-vis biblical text and historical event in a new perspective. If in fact the canonical documents are primarily task-oriented, and if the divine concern is primarily that of functionally equivalent faith responses on the part of the people of God to revelation in its variety of historically mediated forms, then it seems more appropriate to presuppose "proximalist" rather than "precisionist" correspondence and coherence theories of truth with respect to the biblical documents. For example, if it should be asked whether 23 or 24 thousand Israelites fell in a single day, it might be helpful to point out that the intent of both texts is quite likely more concerned with eliciting functionally equivalent responses of obedience than with achieving exact arithmetical precision of reporting. Evangelicals are prepared to admit quite readily the use of approximations by the writers of Scripture. If this recognition could be generalized to apply to other variations on the basis of a theory of approximate coherence

and approximate correspondence—"coherence and correspondence within providentially permitted tolerances of variation"—then perhaps some of the tensions in the contemporary discussions of biblical authority could be overcome.

5. Finally, the concept of contextualization, insofar as it lends to a greater appreciation of the permissible variety which can exist among biblically oriented theologies, has implications for denominational and ecumenical relations. Once we recognize the historicity and contextuality of our own theological tradition, we may be more willing to acknowledge a wider spectrum of other theological traditions as authentic (though, in our judgment, defective) expressions of Christian faith. Though we may choose to draw the boundaries between the essentials and the nonessentials at a different point, we may be more hesitant to label as heretical what may be in fact a permissible contextualization of the faith. Such an outlook could facilitate better relationships between evangelicals and Christians of other theological persuasions.

# Notes to Chapter 11

1. Theological Education Fund Staff, *Ministry in Context,* (Kent, England: Bromley, 1972), p. 20, cited by Wayne C. Weld, "Contextualization," *Covenant Quarterly* 37:1 (1979):29.

2. For representative recent discussions in this vein see Eugene Nida, *Message and Mission: The Communication of the Christian Faith* (Pasadena: William Carey, 1960); *Religion Across Cultures* (New York: Harper and Row, 1968); Jacob A. Loewen, *Culture and Human Values: Christian Intervention in Anthropological Perspective* (Pasadena: William Carey, 1975); William A. Smalley, ed., *Readings in Missionary Anthropology* II (Pasadena: William Carey, 1978); David J. Hesselgrave, *Communicating Christ Cross-Culturally* (Grand Rapids: Zondervan, 1978); Charles H. Kraft, *Christianity in Culture: A Study in Dynamic Biblical Theologizing in Cross-Cultural Perspective* (Maryknoll, NY: Orbis, 1979). The new journal *Gospel in Context* is devoted to issues arising in relation to the contextualization of the gospel. The recent work by Charles Kraft, who teaches at the Fuller School of World Mission, has been especially significant in stimulating my own reflections in this area. A review of Kraft by William Dyrness is forthcoming in *Christianity Today.*

3. See, for example, Daniel von Allmen, "The Birth of Theology: Contextualization as the dynamic element in the formation of New Testament theology," *Int Rev Missions* 64:253 (1975):37–52; William Lane, "[Paul as] Task Theologian," in Barker, Lane, and Michaels, *The New Testament Speaks* (New York: Harper and Row, 1969), pp. 148–49; William L. Lane, "Creed and Theology: Reflections on Colossians," *J Ev Th Soc* 21:3 (1978):213–20. For an able synthesis of the thrust of modern New Testament scholarship, see James D. G. Dunn, *Unity and Diversity in the New Testament: An Inquiry into the Character of Earliest Christianity* (Philadelphia: Westminster, 1977).

4. Bernhard Lohse is probably not overstating the case when he asserts that "modern historical thinking, beginning in the eighteenth century and slowly but increasingly penetrating all areas. . . is one of the greatest movements in the intellectual history of mankind." *A Short History of Christian Doctrine* (Philadelphia: Fortress, 1966), pp. 225–26.

5. It will be suggested that with respect to variant accounts in the synoptic parallels, for example, it might be more helpful to presuppose not a "zero-tolerance" concept of the correspondence and coherence theories of truth, but rather a concept of correspondence and coher-

ence within "providentially permitted ranges of variation"—a concept more in keeping with ordinary language usage.

6. The following statement by Marx is characteristic: "Morality, religion, metaphysics, and all the rest of ideology and their corresponding forms of consciousness no longer seem to be independent... Rather, men who develop their material production and their material relationships alter their thinking and the products of their thinking along with their real existence. Consciousness does not determine life, but life determines consciousness." Marx, "The German Ideology," in *Writings of the Young Marx on Philosophy and Society,* ed. and tr. by L. Easton and K. Guddat (Garden City: Doubleday, 1967), p. 415. On the discipline of the sociology of knowledge, see further Karl Mannheim, *Ideology and Utopia* (New York: Harcourt, Brace, and World, 1936); Kurt Wolff, ed., *From Karl Mannheim* (New York: Oxford Univ. Press, 1971); Peter L. Berger and Thomas Luckmann, *The Social Construction of Reality* (Garden City: Doubleday, 1967).

7. During his earlier involvement with the Religious Socialist movement in Weimar, Germany, Paul Tillich was quite aware of the need for such a self-critical stance in Protestant theology. Theology must continually raise against *itself* the suspicion of ideology. Tillich, "Religiöser Sozialismus II," *Gesammelte Werke.* Bd. 2: *Christentum und Soziale Gestaltung: Fruhe Schriften zum religiösen Sozialismus* (Stuttgart: Evangelisches Verlagswerk, 1962), p. 164. For further discussion, see John Jefferson Davis, *Paul Tillich and Religious Socialism,* Ph.D. dissertation, Duke University, 1975.

On the dangers of an enculturated gospel, see H. Richard Niebuhr, *The Social Sources of Denominationalism* (New York: World, 1957); Martin E. Marty, *Righteous Empire: The Protestant Experience in America* (New York: Dial, 1970); H. Shelton Smith, *In His Image, But...* (Durham, NC: Duke Univ. Press, 1972).

8. Moltmann's statement is illustrative of the mood of that time: "... theological hermeneutics is abstract as long as it does not become the theory of practice, and sterile as long as it does not make 'the entrance to future truth' possible... This hermeneutic can therefore be called a political hermeneutic because it apprehends politics... as the inclusive horizon of the life of mankind." Jürgen Moltmann, "Toward a Political Hermeneutics of the Gospel," in Martin E. Marty and Dean G. Peerman, eds. *New Theology No. 6: On Revolution and Non-Revolution, Violence and Non-Violence, Peace and Power* (New York: Macmillan, 1969), p. 81.

9. Cf. Gustavo Gutiérrez: "Theology as a critical reflection on Christian praxis in the light of the Word... does not stop with reflecting on the world, but rather tries to be part of the process through which the world is transformed." *A Theology of Liberation* (Maryknoll, NY: Orbis, 1973), pp. 13, 15. Jose Miquez Bonino: "The Sociology of knowledge makes abundantly clear that we think always out of a definite context of relations and action, out of a given praxis. What Bultmann has so convincingly argued concerning a *preunderstanding,* which every man brings to his interpretation of the text, must be deepened and made more

concrete . . . Every interpretation of the texts which is offered to us . . . must be investigated in relation to the praxis out of which it comes." *Doing Theology in a Revolutionary Situation* (Philadelphia: Fortress, 1975), pp. 90–91. James Cone: ". . . theology is political language. What people think about God, Jesus Christ, and the church cannot be separated from their own social and political status in a given society." *God of the Oppressed* (New York: Seabury, 1975), p. 45. For evaluations of liberation theologies from an evangelical perspective, see Carl E. Armerding, ed., *Evangelicals and Liberation* (Nutley, NJ: Presbyterian and Reformed, 1977), and David F. Wells, *The Search for Salvation* (Downers Grove, IL: Inter-Varsity, 1978), pp. 119–40.

10. Paul Tillich, *Systematic Theology*, vol. I (Chicago: Univ. of Chicago, 1951), p. 7. Tillich: "Theology moves back and forth between two poles, the eternal truth of its foundation and the temporal situation in which the eternal trust must be received" (p. 3). For an evaluation of Tillich's method of correlation see my article, "Tillich: Accurate Aims, Alien Assumptions," in *Christianity Today*, August 27, 1976, pp. 6–8.

11. ". . . theology can unfold the word only as it deals with an addressed word and very emphatically makes it known in its present significance, in its actuality 'for me.'" Thielicke, *The Evangelical Faith*, vol. I (Grand Rapids: Eerdmans, 1974), p. 24. As Thielicke himself points out, all theologies have addressed their own historical situations. In this sense, contextualization is certainly not a novel phenomenon. In the post-Enlightenment situation, however, the "hermeneutical gap" between biblical text and contemporary context has become a prime methodological problem for theology.

12. Charles Hodge, *Systematic Theology*, vol. I (reprinted., Grand Rapids: Eerdmans, 1975), p. 19. For similar understandings of the nature of theology, see A. A. Hodge, *Outlines of Theology* (reprint ed., Grand Rapids: Zondervan, 1972); A. H. Strong, *Systematic Theology* (Valley Forge: Judson, 1907); L. Berkhof, *Introductory Volume to Systematic Theology* (Grand Rapids: Eerdmans, 1932); H. Orton Wiley, *Christian Theology* (Kansas City: Beacon Hill, 1940); Francis Pieper, *Christian Dogmatics* (St. Louis: Concordia, 1950).

13. David Kelsey, in *The Uses of Scripture in Recent Theology* (Philadelphia: Fortress, 1975), has argued persuasively that it is the theologian's imaginative vision of the "essence of Christianity," rather than exegetical considerations per se, which determines the overall character of the theological system. If Kelsey is essentially correct, as I believe that he is, then creativity, imagination, and novelty are integral to the task of theological reflection. In the field of the natural sciences, Michael Polanyi has demonstrated the essential role played by intuition, personal judgment, and imagination. See Polanyi, *Personal Knowledge: Towards a Post-Critical Philosophy* (New York: Harper and Row, 1964).

14. James Barr, *Fundamentalism* (London: SCM, 1977).

15. Stanley N. Gundry, "Evangelical Theology: Where Should We Be Going?" *Jour Ev Th Soc* 22:1 (1979):11.

16. Carl F. H. Henry, *God, Revelation, and Authority*, vol. I (Waco, TX: Word, 1976), pp. 9–10.

17. Clark H. Pinnock, "An Evangelical Theology: Conservative and Contemporary," *Christianity Today* (Jan. 5, 1979), p. 23.
18. Krister Stendahl, "Biblical Theology, Contemporary," *Interpreter's Dictionary of the Bible* I (New York: Abingdon, 1962), p. 419.
19. This terminology is from David F. Wells, *The Search for Salvation,* pp. 39-40. Wells: "Theology should be concerned to organize doctrines, explore their relations, expose their problems, defend their teaching, relate their content to other fields of knowledge and apply their conclusions to each age in a philosophical and cultural vernacular native to it." "Doctrine" as defined above does not fully reflect the pluriform nature of biblical doctrine (James Dunn), but this is an issue which need not be pursued in relation to the point at hand.
For a similar distinction between "creed" and "theology," see Lane, "Creed and Theology," pp. 214-15.
20. Cf. James Cone: "In order to be Christian theology, white theology must cease being *white* theology and become Black theology by denying whiteness as a proper form of human existence and affirming blackness as God's intention for humanity." *A Black Theology of Liberation* (Philadelphia: J. B. Lippincott, 1970), pp. 32-33. In later works Cone has softened his rhetoric but has not abandoned his insistence that the experience of oppression constitutes an essential hermeneutical *a priori* for understanding the gospel. See *God of the Oppressed* (1975), pp. 39-61. "The Social Context of Theology."
21. E. D. Hirsch, Jr.: "Perspective-effects do not necessarily distort and relativize what we understand. Anyone who takes the perspectivist metaphor seriously is forced by the empirical facts of visual perception to reverse his original inference, and conclude that a diversity of perspectives does not necessarily compel a diversity of understood meanings." *The Aims of Interpretation* (Chicago: Univ. of Chicago, 1976), p. 48. Hirsch's discussion is quite pertinent to current discussions in theological hermeneutics.
22. Michael Polanyi has explored the powers of the human mind to achieve tacit integrations as part of the process of understanding in *Personal Knowledge,* and more recently, in Michael Polanyi and Harry Prosch, *Meaning* (Chicago: Univ. of Chicago, 1975). Polanyi's theory of understanding is derived, in part, from studies in gestalt psychology, as well as from his own knowledge of the history of scientific discovery.
23. G. P. Murdock, an anthropologist, has listed 73 items which appear to be found in all cultures: age-grading, athletic sports, bodily adornment, calendar, cleanliness training, community organization, cooking, cooperative labor, cosmology, courtship, dancing, decorative art, divination, division of labor, dream interpretation, education, eschatology, ethics, ethnobotany, etiquette, faith healing, family, feasting, fire making, folklore, food taboos, funeral rites, games, gestures, gift giving, government, greetings, hair styles, hospitality, housing, hygiene, incest taboos, inheritance rules, joking, kin-groups, kinship nomenclature, language, law, luck superstitions, magic, marriage, mealtimes, medicine, modesty concerning natural functions, mournings, music, mythology, numerals, obstetrics, penal sanctions, personal names,

population policy, postnatal care, pregnancy usages, property rights, propitiation of supernatural beings, puberty customs, religious ritual, residence rules, sexual restrictions, soul concepts, status differentiation, surgery, tool making, trade, visiting, weaning, and weather control. Cited in Kraft, *Christianity in Culture*, p. 87.

24. Hirsch, *The Aims of Interpretation*, p. 39.

25. Dunn, *Unity and Diversity in the New Testament*.

26. See especially Walter Bauer, *Orthodoxy and Heresy in Earliest Christianity* (Philadelphia: Fortress, 1971).

27. James Dunn argues that the Judaizers of the Pauline correspondence were guilty of precisely such a false cultural conservatism, while the apostle Paul risked a fresh contextualization of the gospel in terms of Hellenistic culture.

28. Carl Braaten has recently given the valuable reminder that "... the original matrix of Christian theology is the missionary church." *The Flaming Center: A Theology of Christian Mission* (Philadelphia: Fortress, 1977), p. 13.